CHECKPOINTS AND AUTOSAVES

PARENTING GEEKS TO THRIVE IN THE AGE OF GEEKDOM

CHECKPOINTS AND AUTOSAVES

PARENTING GEEKS TO THRIVE IN THE AGE OF GEEKDOM

DR. ANTHONY M. BEAN, PHD

Leyline Publishing, Inc.
Fort Worth, TX

Book copyright © 2022 by Anthony M. Bean

All rights reserved. No part of this book may be used or reproduced in any manner whatsoever without prior written permission, except for brief quotation of less than one hundred (100) words for reviews and articles.

Leyline Publishing, Inc.
1650 West Rosedale Street, Suite 305
Fort Worth, Texas 76104
www.leylinepublishing.com | www.geektherapeutics.com

Printed in the United States of America
10 9 8 7 6 5 4 3 2 1

Library of Congress Cataloging-in-Publication Data is available upon request.
978-1-955406-13-0 (trade paper)
978-1-955406-14-7 (e-book)

Editing by Anthony M. Bean
Copyediting and Proofreading by Anthony M. Bean
Text Design and composition by Asya Blue Design
Cover Design and Illustration by OLINART
Printed by Versa Press

To my loving wife, Holiday and
my own little superheroes: August and Lulu.

Watching your resilience, perseverance, and growth has been
worth every part of the journey together.

May you always remind me of the best parts of parenting.

Sharing the worlds of Geekdom has been
amazing with you both.

CONTENTS

FOREWORD: GEEK THERAPEUTICS
1

INTRODUCTION
3

CHAPTER 1
THE JOURNEY BEGINS
9

CHAPTER 2
WHAT IS GEEK THERAPY?
25

CHAPTER 3
VIDEO GAMES
43

CHAPTER 4
DUNGEONS & DRAGONS
65

CHAPTER 5
MAGIC: THE GATHERING & OTHER TCGS
83

CHAPTER 6
COSPLAY, LARPING, & FAN FICTION
103

CHAPTER 7
FANTASY & SCI-FI—HEROIC PLAY
123

CHAPTER 8
THE POWER OF ANIME
141

CHAPTER 9
COMIC BOOKS & SUPERHEROES
159

CHAPTER 10
POP CULTURE
179

CHAPTER 11
ESPORTS & STREAMING
197

CONCLUSION
215

GLOSSARY
220

REFERENCES
221

FOREWORD: GEEK THERAPEUTICS

Being a geek can be lonely. There are many who self-identify as "geeks" and struggle to overcome judgement, social isolation, and lack of shared interests with their peers. Historically, geeks have been shoved into dark corners of society, deemed "weird," "nerdy," or "freaks" by people who do not understand them. It can be difficult for a geek to form meaningful connections with others, not because there is anything wrong with them, but because others decide they are not worthy of connection based solely on how they spend their spare time.

I grew up as one of these geeks, and as I made connections in the geek community, I realized the remarkable opportunities that geek artifacts provide for children, adolescents, and even adults. I witnessed a shared experience between geeks that I wanted to replicate for others. I started my company, Geek Therapeutics, with the intention of bringing people together through these innovative, immersive experiences previously sequestered to the geeks of the world.

Although the term "geek" has not completely overcome its negative connotation, there has never been a time more accepting of geeks and geek interests. The time for the geeks to inherit the Earth is upon us, and they need to be supported so they can step out from the dark corners and take their place in the sun.

The rise of cultural normalization has brought some of the most niche artifacts of geek culture into mainstream media and popular culture. Still, there is some mystery surrounding geek artifacts, and people (especially parents) who want to engage with geeks and geek culture have trouble finding a point of entry.

At Geek Therapeutics, clinicians and scholars bridge the gap between geeks, parents, peers, and therapists to create practical and innovative therapy sessions. Geek Therapy encompasses many paradigms of thought, intellectual curiosities, and specialized interests outside of "normal" social conformity. This can range from well-known areas like video games, comic cons, and TV shows to the less well-known topics of board games and verbose fantasy novels. There are clinicians who use these geek cultural artifacts to promote social normalcy, community, reduce anxiety and depression, and help clients understand who they are through their interests.

For more information about Geek Therapeutics, including locations, hours, upcoming events, and supplemental learning materials, visit us online!

www.geektherapeutics.com • hello@geektherapeutics.com

INTRODUCTION

"It's Dangerous to go Alone! Take This."
— The Legend of Zelda, 1986

My alarm is not set to go off for another hour, and there is something lurking in the dark. I am not thinking about the school board meeting, or the deck I need to fix up, or the earnings report at work. Fast asleep, the daunting tasks of the day have not reached me yet. I am completely unaware that through my open bedroom door, an intruder approaches.

A sharp tug rips the blankets from the bed. I shoot up, ready to fend off whatever is hiding in the early morning murkiness. There! I do not see a masked robber or a rabid dog—I see my son. His face is glowing from the backlit screen in his hands. I blink myself into consciousness and as soon as he sees me awake, he shouts, "Dad, come on! We gotta catch Mewtwo today!"

How easy it is to roll over and drift back to sleep. I could bonk him on the head like a snooze button (but gentler) and delay the start to another big day...

But I see his excitement even in the low light and know I cannot bring myself to say no. It would be like saying no to myself, who wanted to play *Pokémon* with his own parents but never had the chance.

So I roll out of bed, scoop him up, and toss him over my shoulder, singing, "Today's the daaaaay!" while he squeals and clutches the game for dear life.

It is not a secret that keeping up with your children can be a challenge. You work hard, make sacrifices, and try to relate to your kids, but it can be an uphill battle when their interests, opinions, and habits change like the seasons. Relating to geeks, though, can be even harder.

Geek culture is more relevant today than it ever has been. Hobbies like *Dungeons & Dragons*, Japanese anime, and *Magic the Gathering* are widespread in popular culture, becoming more mainstream by the year. "Geek" is not the insulting term it was when I was growing up, either. In the twenty-first century, "geek" is a term comic book readers and strategy board gamers use to lovingly describe their lifestyles. With more young people embracing geek culture, parents might pick up the geek torch too to better understand, relate to, and bond with their children's interests.

Not every parent grew up with a geeky lifestyle to draw from. We do not all have a wealth of video games or fantasy movies to "geek out" about when we share them with our kids for the first time. And when we turn to the Internet to learn more about geek culture, the information out there feels esoteric, critical, or confusing. Altogether, connecting with a *Pokémon*-crazed kid is not as easy as helping them with their multiplication tables.

With all the buzz geek culture receives, you would think it would be easy for parents to look up how to connect through their kids' geeky interests, but it is more trying than ever.

We will start with the most pressing questions parents have about video games when their children first show interest in them.

Can video games harm my kids? Is it healthy for children to "role play?" Is this trading card game going to teach my kid a bad habit, like gambling?

Parents have been asking questions like these since the Stone Age. We all want to know whether the next new fad is going to be helpful or harmful to our families. Unfortunately, we have a tendency to overreact in a negative way. The negativity bias is what makes us gravitate towards horrific headlines, remember foul memories profoundly, and fear statistically unlikely disasters simply because they are negative.

This can skew parenting articles about video games and other geeky pastimes in a negative direction. Some bloggers might misinterpret data (on purpose or accident) because they are more focused on the downsides of gaming or role playing. Others latch on to the risks of a new geek trend before they fully understand it, so they write up a dangerous exaggeration or misinterpretation. Parents who resonate with these fears perpetuate them in the comments sections of social media posts, when the fears might be based in misinformation or suspicious anecdotes. You might venture out to these digital scribbles hoping to find educational value, but some of the content will convince you that the game your child is playing at school was produced by the Devil himself.

The quantity of parental information available on the Internet is boundless, but the quality is laughable. Why does geek culture get such a bad rap from some parents, while others embrace it with excitement?

This phenomenon is an example of what Stanley Cohen dubbed the "moral panic" in 1972. Moral panic happens when something new, called a "folk devil," is introduced to a community and invokes a feeling of fear. This fear stems from a potential threat the folk devil seems to pose to the established values, interests, or well-being of the community. Moral panics are generally unproductive because they spur talk of all the negatives ruining our children, but do not encourage people to think about the positives or possible solutions.

Right now, geek culture is a new folk devil on the block. In fifteen years, it will be artificially intelligent butlers, or virtual reality, or whatever new technology challenges our status quo. When these new platforms, gadgets, and activities are operationally defined by someone who does not understand them, misinformation spreads like a virus. The folk devils grow bigger and scarier. They solidify the idea that new trends are temporary, evil deviants we must destroy.

Geek culture is misunderstood, and so are the geeks who love it. When parents view their kids as pariahs for playing Minecraft, this further distances parents from connecting with their kids while making them feel invalidated for what they enjoy. Meanwhile, most parents have not even tried booting up the game themselves to give it a fair shot.

The more we learn about this "folk devil," the more we see how silly it is. A deeper understanding of geek culture actually presents amazing opportunities for parents to engage with children through exciting, creative, and enriching media.

My son and I bond over *Pokémon* together, but we are doing so much more than playing a video game. I see my son comprehending new systems, considering outcomes, and practicing decision making. He knows in the Pokémon system, water-type Pokémon are weak to electric-type attacks, but resistant to fire-type attacks. When he uses his water-type Blastoise against a fire-type Charizard, he knows he has an advantage. When he chooses which attack to use, he has to read the options and think critically, improving his reading comprehension and problem solving. He learns strategies to catch and train his team of Pokémon, celebrating wins and overcoming losses.

Today, we put all those experiences together to go catch a Pikachu!

If you want to parent a geek, get geeky. But what hobbies are "good" to bond over? How can we separate the moral panic from actual threats?

This book will break down the best geek entertainment available for child development. Out of the eight most common engagement opportunities within geek culture, this book will serve as a guide from a research-backed perspective. By the time you reach the last page, you will have a guide to finding common ground with your child that will help you as a parent foster a better relationship, and maybe a new favorite hobby.

CHAPTER 1

THE JOURNEY BEGINS

"Your very own tale of grand adventure is about to unfold."
— Professor Oak, Pokémon HeartGold & SoulSilver

Parenting is a heroic task, and facing unknown threats to our children takes heroic bravery.

Before our children can walk and talk on their own, protecting them from threats is straightforward. Infants are almost always by our side and cannot do much on their own, so most threats to their safety are obvious to us. As our children grow, the way we protect them changes. We try to imprint as many lessons on safety and critical thinking as we can, but we cannot look over our children's shoulders every second of the day, nor should we. So, we tell them how to handle the threats we know about. *Don't touch the hot stove, don't run when the floor is wet, don't drink the "potions" under the sink.* When they are off at school, we remind them to look both ways, bring their jackets, and keep away from strangers, but there are some threats we cannot prepare our children to handle. These unexpected threats could traumatize our kids, and we would have no control over it. This puts all the work we did to prepare them for the world at risk, right?

We have protected our children from expected dangers for years, but the world has changed so much since we were kids, we have massive blindspots in our threat awareness. Every time our children meet us after school, playdates, or sports programs, they are asking about new games, cartoons, and websites. None of them existed when you were growing up (we had a Commodore 64 that played games off of floppy disks) and parenting books have not caught up yet. We try our best to understand *Fortnite, My Hero Academia*, and TikTok to see what threats might reach our children, but we are outmatched.

The folk devil around nerd culture perpetuates misleading information about the trendiest games, cartoons, and websites our kids love. By the time we do get a good feel for a new trend, it is already over and our kids are onto the next one, leaving us wondering why we put in all the time and effort in the first place. Parenting books cannot keep up with every new fad under the sun, yet we must explore unfamiliar landscapes to assess their risks, rewards, and suitability for our kids.

How can we, the heroes, *save the children*? How can we protect against stuff we know nothing about?

We have to overcome the folk devil.

To summarize, the folk devil is fear of the unknown, manifested. In this case, most parents do not understand geek culture so they build a sinister folklore around it, turning it into a folk devil.

For example, when we chatter about the influence of screen time on our kids because we are worried about potential dangers, we can turn screen time into a folk devil. Social media, news cycles, and concerned neighbors stoke our fears with inaccurate claims about technology. A new article published to explain the effects of screen time might pick up a million hits per day on Facebook even if it is full of made-up, self-serving claims. Opinions and unfounded fears ramp up, so parents get on the offensive. Suddenly, parents limit screen time to one hour per week even if research suggests more time as harmless. The fear of screen time grows out of control and creates a folk devil. This can be devastating as some children lose access to social spaces, learning opportunities, or forms of expression, over a rumor.

As humans, we are naturally afraid of the unexpected threats and let those fears grow into general panics, attitudes, and misconceptions. Although it is a natural response to protect our children from potential threats, geek culture is not something to fear.

This book is a friendly guide to help you dismiss the moral panic around geek culture artifacts like video games, animations, and role-playing games. The more we read, the more we learn (as Levar Burton says in *Reading Rainbow*), the more we can dispel irrational fears about geek culture and embrace it for what it is. Even when the trends referenced in this book become outdated, the same lessons can apply to the next generation of nerd culture and folk devils.

MISCONCEPTION 1: VIDEO GAMES CAUSE VIOLENT BEHAVIOR

If you are the parent of a video gamer, it is likely you have heard this rumor: Video games cause violence. Sensationalists might have you believe *Call of Duty* transforms innocent children into aggressive vandals sowing chaos, or screen junkies scrounging for *just one more game, man*. We must put this rumor to rest right now: **video games do not create mass murderers or psychopaths.**

There are quality studies that evaluate the effects of video games on developing minds, but most news articles seen online do not reference them. Instead, they reference studies with questionable methods, cherry-picked data, or a small scope that mistakes molehills for mountains. Proper academic studies take years of retesting and hundreds of participants to produce reliable data. And even with good data, we can jump to inaccurate conclusions.

A common fallacy that influences the way studies' findings get misconstrued is the questionable-cause fallacy, which incorrectly assigns two events or variables a cause-and-effect relationship when they are really only correlated to each other. When two variables are correlated, it means there is some kind of relationship between them. The relationship could be as simple as two trees looking alike or as complex as two people falling in love. Just because two variables are related does not mean one caused the other. *Correlation does not imply causation.* If you stick me in a room with a strawberry while I am wearing a red T-shirt, there is a correlation between me and the strawberry: we both have some red on us! Unless I pick up the strawberry and smash it all over my shirt, that strawberry did not *cause* me to have red on my shirt. The two variables (my shirt and the strawberry's color) are not related through a causal relationship.

Questionable-cause fallacies come from the mind's natural pattern-finding impulse. It works great for murder-mystery authors who want to mislead their readers with red herrings, but it is best left out of science and psychology.

Reliable research on video games has actually revealed a **correlation** between the personality characteristic of aggression and video games: they tend to act as a covariant, or amplifier, for tendencies already inherently displayed in the player. If a player demonstrated aggressive tendencies in personality examinations, he or she also displayed those traits while playing the video game. If a player demonstrated supportive, pacifist behavior, he or she maintained those traits in-game as well. Reliable studies that examine relationships between video games and aggression in players have never concluded video games as a cause of increased aggression in anyone who is not already naturally aggressive.

Similar results appear in other competitive environments like sports games, science fairs, and beauty pageants. Competition, difficulty, and pressure appear to have more of an effect on bringing out aggressive behavior than video games specifically have on participants. So why do we not see as many headlines saying soccer and science fairs cause aggression? We could draw the same conclusion, but usually do not, because sports and science have defeated their folk devils. They have become more socially acceptable than video games.

MISCONCEPTION 2: IT'S JUST A PHASE

Another rumor to combat the folk devil must be debunked: the "It's just a phase" notion. It is important to be open to our children's geeky interests because geek culture is not going anywhere. Science fiction and role-playing have only become more popular over the past few decades and show no signs of slowing down.

Parents watch their kids' interests evolve over the years, so it is easy to consider an interest in comic books or *Dungeons & Dragons* (D&D) as "phases," but this kind of thinking is problematic. When we refer to our child's interest as temporary or "a phase," we devalue their experience. Brushing off our children's interests can make our kids feel unimportant, incorrect, or otherwise undeserving of their parents' attention. Sometimes kids grow out of "geeky phases" because they are tired of feeling ashamed.

When we believe geek culture is a harmful phase, we feed the folk devil. To dodge the unexpected threats we restrict access to certain games, shows, or hobbies until the hazardous phase is "over." However, this does not keep our kids from danger. It tells them we do not trust their judgment and it devalues their experiences, which creates an unnecessary struggle in our power dynamic.

Instead, parents should learn more about their kids' interests so they can help them decide right from wrong. There can be unknown threats in the world of online gaming, like bullies or scammers, but instead of unplugging the router, do some research to make those threats known. Then, like any other known threat, we can teach kids how to handle them. We can model curiosity and openness while we assess a new pastime's safety. In a later chapter, we will take a closer look at online gaming and what every parent needs to know. Dismissing or restricting our children's interests in anime, tabletop games, or other artifacts of geek culture can drive a wedge in our relationships when we could be creating stronger bonds. To protect our children, it is best to engage in geek culture so we can supervise while strengthening our relationships.

MISCONCEPTION 3: GEEK CULTURE MAKES KIDS DISCONNECT

To overcome the folk devil, we must first bust another myth: geek culture makes my kids disconnected and antisocial. Many parents think fantasy worlds can pull their children into isolation, but actually, geek culture is an incredible way to connect.

A few years ago, a young patient of mine (we will call her Lucy) used geek culture artifacts to save her life. Lucy's mother brought her to our nonprofit practice, The Telos Project, because she had been showing some early signs of schizophrenia. At only thirteen years old, this display is concerning enough to merit psychological testing. At the time, she was a small girl with a sinking posture and big, heavy bangs hiding her face. We developed a cold rapport during her two-hour psych evaluation, but when I asked her about the anime characters on her oversized T-shirt, her eyes emerged from under her hair and sparkled with excitement.

"This?" Lucy beamed, "It's *Bungo Stray Dogs*."

"I've never heard of that one," I said with intrigue. "What's it about?"

The two-hour session became three-and-a-half while we chatted about anime together. She mentioned she is the only one in her family who likes anime or plays D&D. She has two sisters at home, but they do not care about her interests. Neither do her parents. She has no one at home to talk to about her passions. While Lucy had been quiet and complacent during our initial session, she became more animated and cheery as we dug into her favorite D&D campaigns and anime characters. I was motivated by her enthusiasm and brought her on as a client to monitor her mental state.

"I have no clue what's going on," her mom said during our first session together. "I don't know what's happening with her, it's like every time I try to engage, she shuts down."

I looked over at Lucy, who shielded her expression behind her hair curtain. It was clear her mom was trying to engage, but Lucy would not open up unless it was on Lucy's terms.

"I'm going to assign you some homework," I told them at the end of the session. "I'm going to show you something you probably saw when you were Lucy's age. It's a show called *Cowboy Bebop*."

"I have seen that before!" Lucy's mom replied.

"Good! Your homework is to watch one episode together tonight."

Lucy perked up and said, "Can we watch more than one?"

"Of course!" I said, "as long as you watch at least one. I'm going to be honest about this assignment: it's a way for you guys to engage with each other. Watch at least one episode together and then have a quick, easy conversation about what you liked and what you didn't like."

Over the next six months of treatment, Lucy blossomed. It turned out her schizophrenic symptoms were actually symptoms of severe depression. Without anyone to talk to or engage with, Lucy felt alone and fell into an unhealthy mental condition. Her thoughts turned suicidal when she gave up on making progress. Instead of using more traditional coping methods to treat her depression, I used her love of geek culture to craft a personalized treatment plan. I believed we could turn her life around with this frame of reference and some encouragement.

In one instance, we used her knowledge of common anime tropes to help Lucy relate to her peers at school. In popular anime shows, there are certain character tropes across the entire genre, repeatedly appearing in almost every anime series. I asked her questions about some of her classmates and asked her, "What type of anime character do you see that classmate as?" Once she picked a trope, I helped her realize she *can* relate to her peers, making it easier to interact with them.

"Yeah," she affirmed, "It does seem like I know how to do it!"

Over the next few weeks, we made incredible progress. By using the tropes she was already familiar with and playing with them to anticipate the needs and interests of her peers, Lucy felt more control over her interactions and was less anxious in group settings. She took the trope concept and ran with it. Before I knew it, she was rescheduling appointments because they conflicted with sleepovers and D&D campaigns with her new friends. By the time Lucy was discharged, she was a completely different girl who watches anime with her family a few nights per week.

After finishing *Cowboy Bebop*, Lucy got to pick the next show they watched together. Her confidence skyrocketed as she felt validated at home, and Lucy's mom learned to better understand and communicate with her daughter. Lucy's mother modeling how to engage in Lucy's interest also prepared Lucy to interact with her peers' interests to form social bonds. Lucy, her mother, and her friends are more connected than ever thanks to anime.

MISCONCEPTION 4: KIDS SHOULD BE MORE PRODUCTIVE

To add another nail in the folk devil's coffin, we can debunk this myth: Geek culture is a waste of time, they should be spending their time on more productive activities.

It is easy to see an unmoving child staring at a screen and think it is a total waste of time, but that is not always the case. They could be playing a highly stimulating *Civilization* game or seeing a tough decision unfold in *Star Trek*. Geek culture is not a waste of time if it teaches real-life lessons that support creativity, confidence, and critical thinking as most (if not all) do. My son and I play *Pokémon* together regularly, and we use it as a learning tool.

When a new Pokémon appears for the first time and my son has not collected it yet—which happens frequently, since there are 898 of them at the time of publishing—the encounter simulates real-life, decision-making moments. On my turns with the controller, I have the chance to model appropriate behavior for my son. I can model a low frustration tolerance and productive critical thinking. When my son plays, he can work through his curiosity and problem solving with an added benefit we do not always have in the real world. Inside a game, there is safe space to F.A.I.L.

F.A.I.L. is an acronym I use for a "Failed Attempt In Learning." Failure is not something we should avoid, because our failures give us the greatest opportunities to learn. When I hear my son say, "I don't know what to do," I recognize his confidence is lacking. He is afraid the wrong move will lead to failure. When we play *Pokémon* together, he is free to press Pause and talk through his choices one at a time. He can talk through his curiosities and frustrations, and I can provide him with validation and acknowledgement. If he gets stuck, I ask him, "What do you think we should do?" and let him

CHECKPOINTS AND AUTOSAVES

develop a critical thought. Here on the pause screen, my son has the opportunity to fail in a safe environment. Children's prefrontal cortices and critical thought patterns are not fully formed yet, so it is beneficial for children's development to have a safe place to make choices and observe how their decisions play out. In a video game, my son can troubleshoot without major consequences, like physical harm. If he fails to catch the Pokémon on the first try, we can pause, reflect, and adjust his strategy for next time. I can also acknowledge and validate his frustration, modeling calmness in a frustrating situation. I can ask questions to help him develop curiosity for his own actions, which helps him develop self-awareness. This controlled arena helps my son practice critical thinking, which translates to more adept and confident critical thoughts in the real world.

The tabletop game, *Dungeons and Dragons* (D&D), promotes the same kind of controlled environment that fosters critical thinking. The concept of the game is for players to create their own characters and to react to situations in the game as their character would. The Dungeon Master (DM, also known as a Game Master, or GM) builds a world and a story based on classic D&D concepts and rules. The story is loose, though, because the players have free reign, and their choices drive the story in all sorts of directions.

D&D presents a freedom of choice to players and makes critical thinking a key component of the game. If D&D seems too complicated for your younger child, why not start with a game like *Knights of Underbed*? In this simple roleplaying game, you and your child play as stuffed animals who protect their sleeping owner from the monsters under the bed. In both games, the DM controls the environment where players operate, and the players challenge their critical thinking to overcome obstacles in unique ways. Geeky games are not a waste of time, they are learning opportunities in a place safe for sandboxing our decisions.

GETTING THE REAL STORIES THROUGH GEEK MYTHOLOGY

Breaking down four common myths around geek culture helps us as parents overcome the folk devil and see geek culture as a teaching and learning tool. Hopefully we can now understand how, while geek culture is not entirely threat-free, we can dive in and help our kids navigate it. It is much healthier to enjoy geek culture with our children than to fear it, dismiss it, or restrict it. So, why does this folk devil exist? Why are there not more parents who see geek culture as more than the scary beast it is made out to be?

Geek culture has been around for decades, but it is still a folk devil to so many people because they do not speak the language. The underlying thread between all these busted myths is simple: when we can speak geek, we get a clearer picture of the culture. We do not need to become an expert geek ourselves, but we can pick up enough of the language to understand its natural ebbs and flows. We can create an opportunity for our children to teach us the language. When we explore geek culture with our children, they can show us it is not all bad, and engaging with it benefits everyone.

To better connect with our children through geek culture, we ought to learn the language. A great way to speak geek is by learning about its mythology.

Take the Marvel Cinematic Universe, for example: ten years of interesting characters and engaging storylines weaving together to create a giant mythology (a mythology that borrows from other mythologies).

When we look at this artifact from a mythological studies perspective, we can see the lessons it portrays. The series teaches important life lessons about friendship, resiliency, family connections, and becoming a personal hero. Every geek culture artifact has a mythos we can relate to our own lives, which makes it a bit easier to learn the language.

According to comparative mythology and religion professor, Joseph Campbell, we are each the hero of our own story and we all navigate through a template of obstacles, antagonists, and cultural struggles. Here are some of the common character tropes we might encounter in life and in mythology[1]:

The Mentor: A teacher or trainer who helps our hero by motivating and protecting them. The mentor helps the hero overcome their fears and prepares them for their journey.

The Threshold Guardian: A character who stops the hero from making progress on their journey. The Threshold Guardian can either be passed or made into an ally. These characters test our hero's personality and commitment to the journey.

The Shadow: These antagonists do not think of themselves as "bad guys," they just want the opposite of what our hero wants. They are often worthy opponents, creating conflicts that test our hero and bring out the best in them.

If these characters seem relatable to your real life, you will have no problem getting to know the characters in your children's favorite mythologies, as distant as they might seem right now. Treating our children's interests like university seminars might not seem like a priority, but it pays off when we are bonding over their favorite shows and connecting in ways we never imagined. For example, we can have deep conversations about character creation.

---

[1] "Subject Guides: The Monomyth (The Hero's Journey): Archetypes." Archetypes - The Monomyth (The Hero's Journey) - Subject Guides at. Grand Valley State University, June 10, 2021. https://libguides.gvsu.edu/c.php?g=948085&p=6857314.

In video games and D&D campaigns, we often play as characters we relate to within the game mythology. Studying the mythologies our children love and talking about which characters they relate to can open a window into their personal stories. Plus, crazy characters and epic backdrops give us a fun way to talk about motivations, values, and fears. We might broach an insightful conversation by asking questions like these:

Did you go for a strength-based character because being strong is a trait you like about yourself? Or is strength a trait you want to have more of?

Did you choose to be a healer because you like to help people in the real world? Do you like being a "supporter" in real life?

Engaging in mythology can remove real-world implications and allow our children to freely reveal their personal priorities, which helps us understand them better.

Some parents might feel overwhelmed by the amount of mythos their children are interested in, especially when our kids consume so much more media than we did at their age. Keeping up with all the stories, games, and YouTube channels our kids interact with on a weekly basis can seem like an impossible task, leaving parents afloat in a sea of game controllers and trading cards.

How do we know where to start?

Well, the first and easiest way is to ask your child. When they are playing a game or streaming a show, ask them what they are doing and whether you can watch. Make mental notes of what you find interesting, and when a break happens, ask a question or two. There is plenty of time to have all your questions answered, so try not to overwhelm them with more than a few at a time. What you are doing is gathering information about the mythology while showing interest in their hobbies. Soon, you will be speaking the language and asking higher level questions, so your child will be more likely to engage and open up.

Not only will engaging your child with questions about a game or series give you more information about the mythology itself, it will also help you understand *why* their favorite mythology is so powerful to your child. Maybe they love watching Hayao Miyazaki's *Spirited Away* so much because the story's hero, Chihiro, spends most of the movie exploring a strange new world on her own. Maybe your child admires Chihiro's sense of freedom and responsibility because they are feeling stifled at home. By giving them more responsibilities at home, one at a time, you can help your child develop a deeper sense of self-sufficiency. Learning through their lens allows you to see where their life feels lacking and make changes to promote growth.

Another way to gain preliminary knowledge about your child's interests is to check the rating. Movies and TV shows are rated by the American Movie Association (AMA), while video games and applications are rated by the Entertainment Software Rating Board (ESRB). The ESRB divides their ratings into three sections: Rating Categories, Content Descriptions, and Interactive Elements. Each section gives details about age appropriateness.

Rating categories can range from E (for everyone) to AO18+ (adults only, eighteen and up.) These rating choices are explained by content descriptors, which note areas of interest or concern for parents. ESRB content descriptors include topics like alcohol/drug references, intense violence or violence references, nudity, and more. The Interactive Elements rating warns about potential interaction risks that *do not* affect the game's rating category, like in-game purchases, unfiltered user-to-user communication, and location sharing.

Checking the rating of a video game or app before allowing your child to play without supervision is a great way to gain immediate knowledge about the game's potential risks. However, just like with movie ratings, it is best not to judge an artifact by the rating alone. Seeing it for yourself, (YouTube videos are the easiest way to view them) or checking with a trusted person who has experienced the content is the best indicator of how it will affect your child.

Do not be afraid to fall forward during the first few engagements with geek culture. You must be willing to be vulnerable with your child and admit ignorance, which can be tough. As parents, we love being the All-Knowing Master of the Universe, but it is okay for our kids to understand we do not know everything. Even Yoda from *Star Wars* admits this, and he lives a lot longer than us! It might be out of your comfort zone to take mythology lessons from your child, but it is a huge step toward building a stronger connection.

And this is only the tip of the iceberg. There is so much value we can draw from geek culture and its mythology as parents.

CHAPTER 2

WHAT IS GEEK THERAPY?

"It is important to draw wisdom from different places. If you take from only one place, it becomes rigid and stale."
— Uncle Iroh, Avatar: The Last Airbender

When I start working with a new client, they are often surprised by the methods I use. Parents bring their children to me expecting me to back up their complaints about geek interests wasting their child's time. When I prescribe an hour of InuYasha as my client's first "homework" assignment, parents feel like they are being played.

Why would I pay to have someone play games and watch shows with my kid? I could do that for free.

You sure can! Do you, though?

Making time for your child's geek interests can feel like going to the gym: it is always a *possibility*. It is easy to say you will do it tomorrow, or next week when you have more time. Then months go by, and even though you are still paying for it, your gym membership has not been used. Even if you go, you become quickly overwhelmed by the different machines and their confusing instructions. There are so many options, and everyone around you seems to already know what they are doing. It can be hard to know where to start.

The reason you keep your gym membership running every month is because you know how important exercise is for a healthy lifestyle. I am sure you also know how important it is to engage with your children. It is easy to push off in our crazy, busy lives, especially before we see the values geek culture has for our kids. When I work with my clients, I begin by making time for their interests and engaging with them right away. Then, I guide my clients and their parents through geek culture together. Geek Therapy uses artifacts from geek mythology to craft real-life, lessons relatable and engaging for geeks.

We must engage in the mythology our children are interested in if we want to engage with them on their level. Every geek culture artifact has a mythology to frame it. Most things in our world are influenced by mythology, too. The ethos of mythology is everywhere. It can be found in religion, social standards, family dynamics, games, school, work, play... all were created out of lessons from one mythology or another.

"Little Red Riding Hood" is a myth created in the late sixteenth century to warn children about venturing into dangerous areas. We might not need warnings about the woods anymore, but we still avoid some of the darker streets on our way home because of modern myths about characters as cunning and vicious as the Big Bad Wolf. Our real-world mythology helps us make choices in our lives, and geek mythology helps the people who engage with it feel connection to one another, make decisions, and gain a sense of importance in their own lives.

Myths have saturated the human race for centuries. We still study intricate, dramatic mythology created by ancient Greeks, Romans, and Norse cultures. Even though we mostly study them for historical significance, some of the stories still contain valuable lessons. "Looks can be deceiving" might have originated as a warning to avoid Zeus, but disguises are a plot device found in any good mystery or thriller story today. Almost every culture between Ancient Rome and modern America created myths to act as a moral compass. Myths create a morality that make us feel like we matter, like we are connected to something bigger than us. Even in our everyday life, outside the pages of a story or channels on our television, mythology is happening all around us.

Mythology from comic books, video games, and roleplaying games are exaggerated versions of our society's personal mythologies. Different games and subcultures engage in mythology in different ways: video games have you act as a hero in someone else's virtual mythology, anime shows a cast of characters making tough decisions in their own mythology via relatable, personal journeys, and *Dungeons & Dragons* (D&D) campaigns use a wide variety of mythologies to create a new one based on the players' choices. When we consume mythologies from different mediums, they expand and influence our morals. Engaging in the same mythology as our clients helps Geek Therapists understand their clients' motivations, hesitancies, and values better. Parents can learn to use Geek Therapy to connect with their children the same way we use it in a clinical setting.

Geek culture is a form of mythology designed to be engaging, entertaining, and educational. In Geek Therapy, we utilize geek culture as a mythological artifact, meaning we separate it from itself and examine it as a cultural item. Take the Marvel Cinematic Universe (MCU), for example: ten years of interesting characters and engaging storylines weaving together to create a giant mythology (a mythology that borrows from other mythologies, like Thor and Loki from the Norse). When we look at this mythology from a mythological studies perspective, we can separate out the lessons it portrays: friendship, resiliency, family connections, saving the world, becoming a personal hero, dealing with loss, grief, depression…the lessons buried in these action-packed films can connect in a multitude of ways to teach important life lessons. And these lessons are delivered through characters with whom your child feels connected.

By using artifacts like the characters in the MCU to frame therapeutic methods, we recognize the client's interest, validate them, and apply those interests to real-life situations. Using this mythological artifact as a framework, we can help clients navigate real world hardships. Ultimately, geek artifacts are pieces of geek interests extrapolated from a myriad of sources.

Artifacts from video games include the overall story, the rules binding the characters, the player's point of view, the game's design, and more. A game like *Mario & Luigi* operates in 2D, but open world games like *Breath of the Wild* are 3D, completely unbound by motion or camera restrictions. These different designs create rules for the characters and stories to follow. We can explore how each of these artifacts contribute to the overall connection we feel within a game while we play as the main character and live in their world.

Artifacts from D&D could be the Game Master's (GM's) flexibility with the players, the campaign style and length, or the quest obstacles. A one-shot campaign completed in a three-hour session might need more events to trigger character growth than a campaign designed to last three months. We can look at how those tests and challenges affect the characters *and* the players, as well as which form of role-playing resonates better with the player.

Media consumption is a large category, but the genres inside often overlap. Artifacts from different types of media can include characters' development, the boundaries of the medium (manga vs. anime vs. live-action movies), and plot devices. For example, time travel is a common plot device capable of being compared across Marvel's *Avengers: Endgame*, comic books like *Mystery in Space*, the *Doctor Who* series, and novels like *The Time Machine*.

This may all seem confusing right now, and there is nothing wrong with that. It can be overwhelming to absorb all the possible applications of geek culture artifacts. Do not be intimidated by the expanse. You do not need to play every video game out there today. You do not need to see every anime show. Once you gather a little information from a few mediums, you will pick up on common tropes and archetypes from geek mythology to carry you through new ones.

For example, The Hero's Journey framework can be applied to *Lord of the Rings* just as easily as the God of War game series. The skill tree in *World of Warcraft* can help you understand deck-building games like *Dominion*. Battling the Elite Four in a *Pokémon* game can prepare you for the duels in *Shadow of the Colossus*. We can take artifacts from geek mythology, extract them from their sources, and apply them to real-world situations to better help our children understand the world as they navigate through it.

I apply the level-up system from role-playing games (RPGs) to my son's life to help him unlock new responsibilities and freedoms. Arbitrary time-locks, like birthdays and New Years, do not magically give experience overnight. Instead of giving him a later bedtime when he reached his fifth birthday, I had my son complete "achievements." He had to set up his backpack for school the next morning and put on his pajamas by himself. These skills helped him gain experience and "level up" to unlock a new bedtime. As he gets older, his achievements will get more difficult, but they will also offer him more freedom. The level-up method uses an artifact of geek culture to help my son understand his role in his personal growth.

The Geek Therapy card deck uses common artifacts from video games, movies, tabletop role-playing games (TTRPGs), comics, and pop culture to help parents recognize these artifacts to communicate with their kids. These artifacts frame different types of therapeutic strategies that improve thought, build insight, motivate, and de-stress clients. Here is an example of a card from the deck:

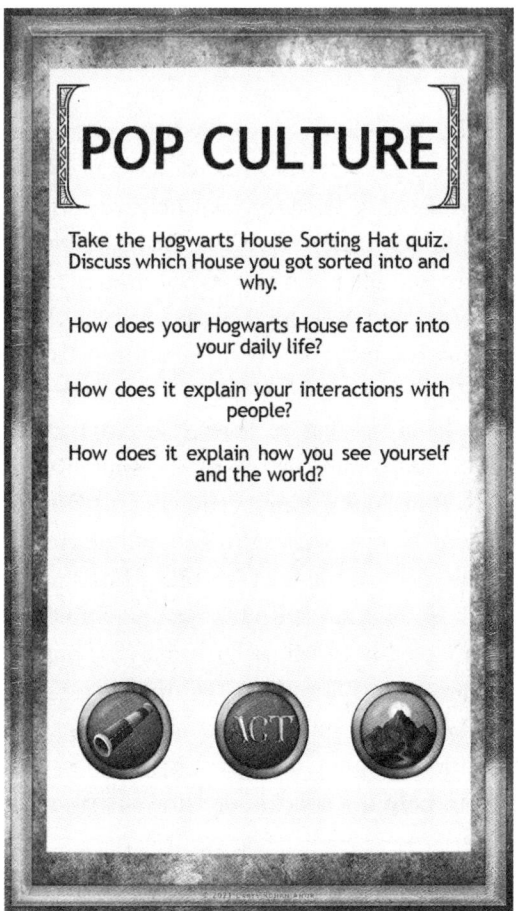

**Pop Culture (Perspective Taking, Acceptance
& Commitment, Self-Exploration)**

When you or your child see this card, *Harry Potter* might immediately jump out at you. You might think, "Oh, I know that one! I have a connection to that, I can resonate with it." Chances are, if you are a *Harry Potter* fan, you've already got some idea of which House you are in—or which House you *want* to be in. Even this slight change is enough to provoke a thoughtful, engaging conversation about personality types. Then, you can expand on the feelings the cards evoke. Were your results different from the last time you took it? Were you disappointed or excited by your House? If you were going to go from Slytherin to Ravenclaw, what would you have to change about yourself? We engaged in a shared interest, and now we have endless opportunities for interpersonal development.

There are more versions of our card deck available to clients, parents, therapists, and other people interested in Geek Therapy. We have spent years developing our unique form of clinical psychology to help people relate to situations in their lives through the lens of geek mythology. I have been using Geek Culture since 2006 to improve mental health in my clients. Before then, I was nothing more than a fellow geek with a dream....

GEEK THERAPEUTICS ORIGIN: THE VIDEO GAME DOCTOR IS BORN

It all started during my time as an undergraduate at Framingham State University (FSU), from 2004 to 2008. FSU towered over the city, perched atop the 282-foot high Bare Hill. The lights from buildings on the outskirts of Boston could be seen on nights with clear skies, only a few miles to the East.

I was working on my bachelor's degree in Psychology, but I also knew how to have a good time. I played *a lot* of Dance Dance Revolution (DDR). When my DDR mats finally bit the dust, my buddies and I came up with the brilliant idea to start a DDR club at the college. By officially forming a club and electing a President, we had the opportunity to petition the college for club funding. We pitched, and they accepted—which meant we now had the money for nice, metal DDR pads, and we could use college classrooms, desks, and projectors for our "meetings." Not much time passed before we started bringing our other consoles with us and expanded our DDR nights into video game nights.

What started as a group of guys playing DDR quickly exploded into an all-out party two to three times a week. Our twelve members shot up to 200. We took over five classrooms at a time, with DDR running in one room, *Mario Kart: Double Dash!!* in another, and rooms with more consoles than I had ever seen in one place before. People brought all kinds of food and drinks from across campus.

I had an epiphany at one of these parties. As I looked around at the sea of people laughing, shouting, and eating the food they had brought, I realized we had formed a community around gaming. It did not matter what major we studied, or what background we came from, we all had this shared experience to bond over. Some of the people in the club were international students who barely spoke English, but we used the video games as a shared language—a laugh erupting from someone tripping off a DDR mat or a cheer after defeating a difficult boss sounds the same in every language. We could resonate with one another and feel like we were connected. Like we mattered.

I was intrigued by how our community formed over a mutual love of video games, and I decided to do what any scientist does when they find intriguing results: repeat the experiment. I wanted to know if people could connect this way outside of a college setting. I could feel there was something special about our geeky interests and our desire to bond, but I needed to prove it.

After graduating in 2008, I dove right into researching video games and their effects on our minds. I published many of my findings in well respected, peer reviewed journals. My study on video game aggression and a study I conducted to map Big Five Inventory (BFI) elements of video gamers across video game genres were just two of my main publications at this time. These studies, as well as others I piloted, will be explained in more detail as we move through different geek culture mediums in later chapters.

When I moved into clinical psychology work, I was motivated by my research and continued exploring the effects of video games. I expanded my practice to include other facets of geek culture as well. I started with clients who had never touched a video game before, and through different mythologies—like fairy tales or classic Greek mythology—I created a gateway through which they understood these stories' effects on our lives. When a client came in knowing nothing about video games, I could trace back their familiarity with other mythos. Instead of playing *Dragon Age: Origins* together, we would start with "The Boy Who Cried Wolf" and work our way up to more complex and relevant mythos.

By using stories my clients heard growing up, we were able to connect on a wavelength separate from the real world. Sometimes a degree of separation from reality makes discussing trauma, addiction, and self-exploration a little easier. Once my clients were comfortable operating from a safe and separate distance, I would introduce them to video games, anime, or fanfiction, depending on what parts of mythology they liked the most. Using geek mythology as scaffolding, I could better relate to my clients. Clients started getting better at a faster pace, and my rate of success was greater than traditional, clinical treatment. This was especially true with my addiction patients.

Traditional success rates for addiction caseloads in the late 2000s were between 5 and 8 percent. After using Geek Therapy for one year, my success rate skyrocketed to 30 percent. These were addicts of all ages and from different walks of life. My oldest client was a 72-year-old man struggling with a heroin addiction. We talked about what myths he was familiar with, and found his gateway in Herman Hesse's fairy tales. Many of Hesse's stories follow the Hero's Journey structure. We talked about tricksters, shadows, and threshold guardians that prevented Hesse's heroes from completing their journeys. Once my client had a solid grasp of the Hero's Journey framework, we used it to explore his monomyth. We framed his life as a hero's journey in the making, and talked about how his addiction disrupted his progress. He saw his addiction as a threshold guardian, blocking his path forward by convincing him he was unworthy of progressing to recovery. He felt empowered by our concept and used it to defeat his personal threshold guardian. He eventually curbed himself off of heroin completely (with additional help from methadone, but the medication only curbs physical withdrawal symptoms and not mental addiction), and was released from care as a healthier man. Seeing the mythology from other stories with happy endings gave him hope that he could persevere through his monomyth, which was crucial to his success.

Each client I see uses geek mythology in different ways for personal improvement. The client is an expert on their own life, so we as clinicians must be experts on how to work their unique experience into a personalized program designed to help them. Not all clients know they are the hero of their own story. Sometimes they need a reminder that they are the master of their own fate, and we are the wise sages guiding them forward.

When we help a client understand their own agency in their life through a "hero" metaphor, we help them feel like they matter. They start to understand the cause-and-effect relationships: their daily chores might feel daunting and counterproductive to their overall journey, but *Iron Man* does not conduct business from a messy Avengers Tower! If he did not take time to clean up after himself, he would never find his suit in time to save the world. There is some magic in the act of playing the hero, so why not extend the same magic into the real world?

Some people, upon realizing their role in their story, discover they have been waiting for a hero instead of acting as their own.

This is especially true for clients with autism and neurodivergent thinking patterns. Some of my clients have admitted they have been waiting for someone to come "save them" from their autism. They view it as a curse, so we take the negative feeling and acknowledge it by saying, "It seems like you feel like your autism is a negative influence in your life. That sounds like it's really difficult for you. What if it's one of your superpowers instead of a super weakness?" Then, we work to reframe their experience through heroic mythology.

Instead of a curse, I challenge my clients to think of their autism and neurodivergent thinking as a superpower. Viewing themselves as a version of their favorite superhero gives them agency and helps them grasp their complex wants and needs better. We explore what strengths their superpower gives them, like super focus or super comprehension. We also discuss their "kryptonites," concepts or objects that make them feel powerless or trapped. By comparing the boundaries of their autism to the boundaries superheroes operate in, they can see how creative problem-solving can help them overcome obstacles and thrive.

After a few years in a clinical setting, word spread about how Geek Therapy results were proving to be unique and consistent. I had requests for presentations multiple times a week. Before long, I spent so much time presenting my research and methods, I ran out of time to actually work with clients. I recruited some other clinicians and researchers to start offering training courses as a placeholder, but we knew the few of us carrying this project forward would soon burn out. I decided to legitimize through incorporation, and thus, Geek Therapeutics was born.

We have given talks across the globe to raise awareness about our results in the field of psychology and medicine. And we are not the only ones recognizing the benefits; the Food and Drug Administration (FDA) approved its first video game as a prescription for ADHD in 2020. The video game, called *EndeavorRx*, was built to improve attention function in children eight to twelve years old.[2] Children feel more connected to content when it is built to engage them on their level, and Geek Therapy helps us meet them on their terms and elevate their personal growth.

GEEK THERAPY IN ACTION

Geek Therapy involves studying the rules of geek mythologies and intentionally breaking out of them into real-world applications. Other forms of therapy use similar techniques: art therapy involves studying symbols and visual cues, and relating them to human experience. We are simply switching a bowl of fruit for dungeon treasure and extrapolating its relationship with our lives, creating permeating changes.

RELATE TO EXTRAPOLATE

As Swiss psychiatrist Carl Jung would have said, geek mythology is a "window to the soul." Jung uses this term when referring to creative expression as a way to understand its creator. Geek mythology is a collection of creative expressions like stories, characters, rules, and structures. We can use it to gain insight into the creator *and* the participant by asking questions like, *How is their world created? How does geek culture engage them? How do they engage with it?*

For example, a therapist I am currently training has a client who loves *Pokémon*. In most *Pokémon* games, the main character starts as a low-level trainer and works their way up to Pokémon Champion. By training their Pokémon to compete against other

---

[2] Commissioner, O. of the. (n.d.). *FDA permits marketing of first game-based digital therapeutic to improve attention function in children with ADHD*. U.S. Food and Drug Administration. Retrieved November 20, 2021, from https://www.fda.gov/news-events/press-announcements/fda-permits-marketing-first-game-based-digital-therapeutic-improve-attention-function-children-adhd.

trainers' Pokémon, they advance in the Pokémon League, facing down eight powerful trainers called gym leaders along the way. Gym leaders operate more as senseis than opponents; they encourage the main character to show what they have learned, and after being defeated they applaud the main character and acknowledge their growth. Respect for *Pokémon* and their battles unite all trainers, and this therapist used her knowledge of Pokémon trainers and gym leaders to frame an activity for her client.

She asked him who he thinks the "gym leaders" in his life are. "Who supports you? Where do you rank among the gym leaders in your life?"

Generally, there are eight total gym leaders in each *Pokémon* game, with some more notable games, like *Pokémon Legends Arceus*, switching to the concept of "nobles" over gym leaders. Each award the main character with a badge upon defeat. Once the main character collects all eight badges, they can challenge the Elite Four trainers in that particular Pokémon League. Only after beating the Elite Four can they try for the title of Champion by challenging the previous winner.

The boy listed some "gym leaders" in his life: his mom, his sister, his best friend, his cousin. He told his therapist these people supported him and helped him gain enough experience to move up in life. His gym leaders could help him become a "master" in his own life just like the ones in *Pokémon* help the game's playable character. He even added a few of his favorite teachers to his lineup when he realized how they help him too. He knew once he became the Champion, his gym leaders would support him and help him maintain his success.

The "gym leaders" framework helped the client understand mutually beneficial relationships and the importance of empathy for people in his life. His therapist used the "window" of Pokémon to communicate with him. She used the gym leader hierarchy as an artifact from the game and broke out of it to apply it to the real world. Gym leaders were not designed to help children understand their relationships with others, but she used the concept to engage and empower her client.

I use artifacts from *Pokémon* as a window into my clients as well. I have a small, stuffed pokéball I use with clients struggling with anxiety. We spend the first half of our session drawing out some of their anxieties and fears. Then, we hang the pictures on the wall. They toss the pokéball at their drawing and "catch" their anxiety. Following the rules of *Pokémon*, they are now in charge of their anxiety and they can train it to work for them instead of against them. This exercise gives them a feeling of control, and empowers them to keep working toward completely overcoming their fears.

MOVING OBSTACLES

Geek Therapy can help clients overcome obstacles as if they are literal barriers straight out of the client's favorite mythos. The obstacle could be a sleeping Snorlax in the road we must move or go around, or it could be a more complex problem we cannot overcome without a new skill. In *Kingdom Hearts*, the main character, Sora, travels past dozens of treasure chests he cannot access until he learns the skill "Glide" from Tinker Bell in Neverland. We can take these obstacles and look at them in real-life from a mythological standpoint.

> *I understand your fight with your parents was really upsetting for you. I wonder, what do you think we need to overcome this obstacle? Is there a skill we must learn before we try talking to them about it again?*

The client might realize they need to work on staying calm during arguments, so we practice some appropriate skills to help them grow. We acknowledge the obstacle, think critically, and overcome it.

Obstacles are not problems, they are opportunities. The challenge comes in the form of a question: *How do we move this out of our way?* We want to collect that new skill or find a secret path to lead us over, under, or around. Obstacles give us a chance to slow down and use our critical thinking skills to progress. When we have an unusually difficult time figuring out how to overcome obstacles, we can figure out why. Are we being held in place by magic? Is there a fear spell keeping us from seeing the solution? Once we understand obstacles better through framework built on geek mythology, we develop our ability to see real-world obstacles in a clearer, more memorable way.

CONSTELLATING

When we use geek mythology in a therapeutic context, it is not enough to stay on the surface of the material. Asking your child, "Which Spider-Man from *Into the Spider-Verse* affected you the most?" is not thought-provoking. The question is unclear and does not take advantage of the deep, introspective opportunities geek mythologies offer.

I use *Into the Spider-Verse's* mythos with my clients, but I dig deeper. I prompt them, saying, "There were a lot of different representations in that movie. Let's take every Spider-character and rank them from favorite to least favorite." After they finish ranking, we discuss their choices.

"I see you ranked Spider-Gwen above Spider-Pig. What about Spider-Gwen connected with you?"

We can start simple and continue to ask questions that explore what they like and do not like about geek artifacts. The more information we guide out of our clients, the more we can understand them and help them understand themselves. Our client might know they liked Spider-Gwen more because she is a person and not a pig, but upon further inspection, we might discover he really connected with Spider-Gwen's grief over losing her best friend. Making connections like these is called constellating: gathering information and connecting it.

When *Black Panther* first came out, some of our Black clients *and* therapists had complicated relationships with the movie. They discovered the toll their lack of representation in superhero mythos took on them. Some were thrilled to finally have someone who looks like them in a lead role, but others were reminded of how long they had gone without it. Some did not realize how important it was to them until it happened. We got to explore all of their emotions together through constellating.

Constellating helps clinicians discover what resonates with our clients and reflects their life. Representation plays a huge role in what makes mythology exciting for engagement. Sometimes our constellations do not match up: I might ask a client if their love for *Lord of the Rings* comes from a longing for adventure, and then get the response, "No, I'm not really the adventurous type." We keep trying, we keep exploring clients' favorite mythologies until we find a concept that resonates. They discover patterns in their own life they never noticed. They find relief and a path for progress in the constellation.

These are just a few examples of simple exercises we use in a clinical setting. Parents and their kids often explore geek mythology and create totally new therapy exercises personalized to their shared interests. We are always excited to hear about new engagement activities that did not occur to us, and we hear about them all the time! However, before we can start developing revolutionary engagement activities for our geeks, we still need a better understanding of geek culture. Specifically, we must explore some of the most popular mediums of geek culture and how we can use them to engage our children.

In the television series *Avatar: The Last Airbender*, the main character, an airbender named Aang, begins his journey as a twelve-year-old child with limited knowledge of the world and his place in it. He has to master control of the four elements: water, fire, earth, and air. He spends four years training and overcoming personal obstacles. Through patience, perseverance, and support from his friends, he ends his journey as the most powerful being in the world. By picking up this book and showing interest in your child's geek pastimes, you have decided to embark on your own training journey. You may not feel like you're an expert in geek culture yet, but before long, you might find yourself cosplaying as the Cabbage Man. (But that is a story for a later chapter.)

Our adventure into the world of geek culture begins on Level 1: video games.

CHAPTER 3

VIDEO GAMES

"Don't wish it were easier, wish you were better."
— Chief, Animal Crossing: New Horizons

I love video games. I also know video games are deemed as one of the most problematic artifacts of Geek Culture. Some children have problematic gaming patterns. Some use gaming as a replacement for other forms of socialization. Some use gaming time as a form of escapism without adequate boundaries. Some players face choices in video games they know should not be replicated in the real world. However, video games themselves are not the problem. The education *around* video games and certain problematic use is what leads to sensationalized articles and feeds a folk devil.

Parents develop a fear of video games because we think they will corrupt our kids. Yes, there are risks involved with allowing your child to play video games, but no more than you would find letting them walk to the grocery store. The reason we blow our fear of gaming out of proportion is because we lack the knowledge to understand their pros and cons. Since lack of knowledge drives the fear, learning about the language gamers share can help us better communicate with our gamer kids through their lens. With a better understanding of gamers and the video games they play, we will feel ready to engage when a gaming opportunity arises.

WHAT ARE VIDEO GAMES?

A **video game** is any user interface or program reliant on human interaction to generate visual feedback. These user or player interfaces can be keyboards, mice, or controllers that allow movement within the virtual reality landscape. Usually, the player gains a sense of accomplishment from playing the game and finishing tasks, quests, and objectives. Progress might look like a new video clip (or cutscene), like the reveal of Batman's nemesis, or a new level unlocked, like a more intricate puzzle in Candy Crush. Video games can be played through many different devices: phones, tablets, Personal Computers (PCs), and consoles like the XBOX, the Playstation, and the Nintendo Switch.

Since the dawn of video games with Pong in 1972, they have become part of our culture. They have progressed in concept, media, storylines, and social interactions due to advancements in technology and popularity among players. Pong's simplistic, vertical movement controls allowed gamers to play two-dimensional ping pong, passing a ball back and forth across a small, black screen with white paddles.[3] This 1-bit game evolved into the 3D rendered games we see today, packed with real-time events and player avatars from around the world. Today, we have games dedicated to space exploration—*Eve, Mass Effect, Super Mario Galaxy*—running on millions of lines of code. Compare that to the ~145,000 lines of 16-bit code Margaret Hamilton submitted to make space exploration a *reality* when she coded the Apollo 11 Guidance Computer. Even the video games on our smartphones are complex and more computationally demanding than the technology man used to step on the moon. The progression of video game technology is astounding and allows the industry to expand

---
[3] Kent, S. (2001). "And Then There Was Pong". Ultimate History of Video Games. Three Rivers Press. ISBN 0-7615-3643-4.

its plethora of stories, play styles, and virtual environments to attract a wider audience.

STYLES OF PLAY

There are two main distinctions in video games that determine style of play: the perspective of the player and how the player interacts with their environment. These factors contribute to the avatar's freedoms, the environment's design, and the player's immersion and presence in the virtual world.

The primary perspectives used in today's video games are detailed in this table:

CHECKPOINTS AND AUTOSAVES

Perspective	Type	Video Game Examples
2D Perspective Avatars move on the left-right and up-down axes. Environment and characters exist as flat illustrations	**Top Down** Also referred to a "bird's eye view," the camera angle is directly above the avatar	Sim City, Railroad Tycoon, The Legend of Zelda (NES), Pokémon
	Side Scrolling The camera flanks the avatar from a fixed angle. The environment "scrolls by" as the avatar moves through it	MegaMan, Double Dragon, Sonic, Super Mario Bros.
3D Perspective Avatars move on the left-right, up-down, and near-far axes. The avatar and the environment have three-dimensional depth and freer, more fluid movement	**1st Person** The player views environment through the avatar's eyes	Doom, Quake, Flight Simulators, Bioshock
	2nd Person The camera is elevated and behind the avatar, allowing the player to see over the avatar's shoulder	Resident Evil 4, Gears of War, F-Zero
	3rd Person Camera is behind avatar, player can see its entire body and surrounding features	Tomb Raider, Super Mario 64, World of Warcraft

The various perspectives in video games are combined with different methods of play to create in-depth interactions.

The three main methods of play motivate the player to complete quests, assume character roles, and work with other players or avatars to progress through the game. The methods of play are described in the table below: [4]

Method of Play	Description of Play Style
Player Versus Environment (PvE)	Players interact with Artificial Intelligence (AI), Non-Player Characters (NPCs), and/or human companions in order to start or complete a quest or storyline scenario.
Player Versus Player (PvP) Also known as "Battle Royale"	Players focus on battles and conflict in the video game between two or more live participants through an interactive, multi-player interface. Usually requires internet or a local connection.
Role-Playing (RP)	Players assume the role of their avatars while exploring the virtual world, similar to how an actor acts out a part in a play or movie.

By understanding the different perspectives and methods of video games, we can pick up on which games our kids like to play and how they interact. Recognizing *Call of Duty* as a first-person shooter in a PvP environment lets you know your child is playing rounds against real people on the other end. They might be chatting with people they already know, or developing new relationships with other gamers through shared goals and interests. It also means the matches cannot be paused because they are live events, so they might not be able to come to the dinner table until the match is over or else they will leave their teammates hanging. We can use this gathered information to predict how different types of video games could influence our children's behaviors.

PREVALENCE IN SOCIETY

A 2008 Pew Research study suggests over 97% of youth play a form of video games, whether on their phone, home-based console, or computer.4 However, video games are not exclusive to young players. Some adults use the video games for cognitive stimulation to stave off dementia or maintain levels of critical thinking during uneventful life periods.

Further, video games can be used almost anywhere for any amount of time. Gamers will settle in for a fun night of *Player Unknown's Battleground* (PUBG) with their buddies or pass time in the doctor's waiting room with *Toy Blast*. Accessible communities and portable devices allow for ubiquitous gaming opportunities for those with disabilities, and it continues to grow every day.

Newer technologies like augmented reality and virtual reality will only increase the prevalence of video games. Augmented reality got its big start with *Pokémon GO!*, in which players see digital Pokémon overlaying their real-world environment when they hold up their phones. Virtual reality headsets are available

---

[4] Lenhart, A., Kahne, J., Middaugh, E., Rankin Macgill, A., Evans, C., & Vitak, J. (2008). Teens, Video Games, and Civics: Teens' gaming experiences are diverse and include significant social interaction and civic engagement. Washington, DC: Pew Internet & American Life Project.

in most retail stores, boasting bone-chilling horror games and breathtaking swims with dolphins from the comfort of your living room. Video games are becoming more popular every year (with no signs of slowing down) and it is vital we understand them so we can use them to our benefit.

It is understandable if video games encompassing parts of our society seems frightening. Relatively speaking, video games have not been around for a long time, so there is much to learn about how to use video games to help us, not hurt us. We can combat the fear of a new culture tool with research and ensure we promote only the best practices.

VIDEO GAMES: VILLAIN OR HERO?

MISCONCEPTIONS ABOUT VIDEO GAME AGGRESSION

Previously, we discussed research claiming video games cause aggression, which is a result of biased and debunked data. We are going to go more in depth about the origins of these claims and how we can correctly interpret collected data. There are no significant links between violent video game play and real-world violence. Thousands of studies have been conducted and no well-recognized study has shown significant links between video games and aggression or violence.

Sometimes, subjects playing video games in a study can show temporary signs of increased aggressive tendencies, but this is not a result of the gameplay itself. A study using the "hot sauce paradigm" asked subjects how much hot sauce they would put on the sandwich of someone who does not like hot sauce. They mostly answered, "none," because they did not want to upset the person getting the sandwich. Then, after playing an hour of *Grand Theft*

Auto (GTA), they were asked again. Some subjects changed their minds and added hot sauce to the sandwich.

The hot sauce paradigm study set out to show a relationship between video games and violence. It revealed that video games temporarily increase aggression because of the subject's low frustration tolerance. The ability to deal with frustrating situations, or **frustration tolerance**, varies among individuals. Those with lower frustration tolerance manifests their upset feelings through aggression more easily.[5] Some video games can be extremely frustrating, especially fast-paced, erratic games. It is similar to playing dodgeball, except everyone has unlimited balls to throw and their gymnasium is burning down. There is a lot happening during these games, requiring dexterity, sharp perception, and the ability to multitask from players to accomplish goals. Repeating in-game deaths and mission failures gets frustrating, but missing the mark in *GTA* is just as frustrating as it is in *Tetris*. The inclusion of in-game violence does not increase a person's frustration, but repeat failures do.

I use video games to work on building frustration tolerance with my clients. A great game to use for this is *Mario Kart*. I let my client start a race, get through their first three laps, and then right before they cross the finish line, I shut off the console.

(Disclaimer: do not try this at home unless you want a broken TV.)

I have had clients scream, yell at me, and smash controllers into the ground. Once they calm down, we have a discussion about it. I acknowledge their frustration and say, "Now, how are we going to handle this feeling?" We calm down together and then we do it again. And then we do it *again*. After a few "failed" races, they might throw up their hands or roll their eyes, but my controllers stay intact and my office TV does not shatter.

---

[5] Przybylski, A. K., Deci, E. L., Rigby, C.S., & Ryan, R. M. (2014). Competence-impeding electronic games and players' aggressive feelings, thoughts, and behaviors. *Journal of Personality and Social Psychology, 106*(3), 441-457. https://doi.org/10.1037/a0034820

"Wow, you really seem to be improving," I say. "Now that we feel more comfortable with our frustration here, how can we improve our frustration at home?"

Instead of avoiding video games that can make our children frustrated, we can use video games artifacts to build frustration tolerance and overcome feelings of aggression. Not only will video games *not* make your child aggressive or violent, video games can help us work through our frustration in a controlled environment. Then, we can recognize it, address it, and overcome it to apply it in real-world situations.

Not everything we learn in video games can be applied to the real world, though. A common debate among video gamers' parents is whether video games with guns are teaching their children to apply sharp shooting in real life.

Have no fear: video games are not substitutes for military-grade training.

Shooter games are designed to *simulate* real-world situations in a fun, engaging way. No video game is going to realistically simulate the throes of war to encourage players. Even games like *Call of Duty*, which are designed to simulate war, account for so much "assistance" that no one shooting a Kilo 141 in-game would recognize how to load a one in real life. Anyone who has experienced life in the military can tell you how vastly different real battle is from the ones you fight from your living room.

In an interview with IGN, U.S. soldiers discussed how games like *Call of Duty: Modern Warfare 3* and *Battlefield 3* compared to their own experience in combat.[6] They unanimously agreed these types of games are completely unrealistic. They discuss how the games allow players to break cover to shoot enemies, leave their team and venture off alone, and collect seemingly endless stores of ammunition. None of these practices happen in real combat.

---

[6] Thang, Jimmy. "What Do Real Soldiers Think of Shooting Games?" IGN. IGN Entertainment, February 23, 2012. https://www.ign.com/articles/2012/02/23/what-do-real-soldiers-think-of-shooting-games.

However, when the Sandy Hook massacre occurred, headlines flooded news feeds, claiming the shooter played video games like *Left 4 Dead*, *GTA*, and *Doom*, which made him an expert in violence. The police raided the shooter's Playstation hard drive and did find a few violent video games, but they all had less than four hours of play time logged.[7] There *was* a video game with hundreds of logged hours in his home: *Dance Dance Revolution* (DDR). Family and friends of the shooter attested to his interest in DDR and stated that although he used to meet up with friends to play, he had been isolating himself in the months leading up to the Sandy Hook shooting. His social isolation is suspected to have been a motivator for his violent crimes, more so than his obsession with an electronic dance game.

Video games alone do not increase violence or aggressive tendencies in youth. That myth is widespread but untrue. When we use video games in a therapeutic setting, we can take some of the most frustrating artifacts from video games, separate them for analysis, and use them to improve, which is an invaluable experience for childhood development.

SOCIALIZATION THROUGH GAMING

Some parents see their unmoving kids plopped before a screen for a few hours and think their children are wasting time. These parents are not looking beyond their child's posture to see what happens in the game.

We can use school as an analogy: someone looking through the window of a classroom is going to see twenty or thirty kids staring at the front of a room for hours at a time, breaking only

---

[7] Sedensky, Stephen J. *Report of the State's Attorney for the Judicial District of Danbury on the Shootings at Sandy Hook Elementary School and 36 Yogananda Street, Newtown, Connecticut on December 14, 2012*, n.d. https://web.archive.org/web/20131125212413/http://www.ct.gov/csao/lib/csao/Sandy_Hook_Final_Report.pdf.

to bury their heads in their books or their writing. If the viewer does not know the children are learning while they sit in rows of a classroom, they might assume school is a waste of time. Under the lens of Zoom schooling, brought to us by the COVID-19 pandemic, students sitting in a virtual classroom appear mistakably close to children sitting in front of a video game. Watching screen does not equate to time wasted. In fact, your child learns more from video games than you might imagine.

Through gaming, many children maintain online friendships. People young and old have developed close-knit friend groups through online platforms since American Online Instant Messenger (AIM) chat rooms in the 1990s. Online friendships are distinct because they operate under an extra degree of separation from the real world. Most online gamers use made up usernames and cartoon avatars for their profiles. They do not have to look presentable to hang out with their online friends. This ability to hide features encourages some online gamers to have meaningful, deep discussions with their online friends. Like the Wizard of Oz, they are operating behind a curtain that protects them from feeling vulnerable in face-to-face situations. When your child allows themselves to be vulnerable with their online friends, they form deep, emotional bonds. And they are not alone: lots of gamers have great friends they have never met in person.

In 2018, A group of six gamers who met online got together for the first time when one member received a terminal cancer diagnosis. He was moved to a hospice center and the other members gathered to visit him. His friends showed up to support him, even though they had never met him in real life. Their friendship of five years felt as real as any other friendship; the minute detail of not knowing each other in-person did not diminish their bonds. It also did not stop them from making friends they *did* know in person. Their "real-world" social skills were not affected by video games or by their online relationships, and likely, neither will your child's.

Although, not every person your child "meets" online is going to be friendly, the same way not everyone your child meets at school or the park will be his friend. Any social environment poses risks for children and parents alike; parents must exercise caution for online strangers like we would for strangers we meet on the street. There are practices we can put in place to mitigate online risks.

Parents might worry about who our children are talking to through their headsets, but we can put ourselves at ease by supervising online conversations and talking to our children about internet safety. Playstation and XBOX systems allow message reports to be sent to parents through their privacy settings. Start by educating your child on internet etiquette. Remind them not to put their real name, birthday, or age in their online usernames. Express how important it is not to disclose personal information to strangers they meet virtually. Keep their profile pictures as characters they love and not their real face (no matter how cute it is!). By teaching our children guidelines for internet safety and supervising games with chat functions, we can encourage them to make healthy friendships and avoid dangerous ones.

Although we worry our children might waste away in front of their video games without any friends or romance, human connection exceeds face-to-face interactions. Our children are wonderful little people and they can make friends wherever they go, even when they are facing a screen at home.

MISCONCEPTIONS ABOUT VIDEO GAME ADDICTION

How much time playing video games is too much? Am I enabling an addiction by letting my kid play *LEGO Batman* after dinner? That is the million dollar question parents want the answer to when they start learning about their child's video game hobby, and the answer is not clear-cut. Every child has a different propensity for forming an addiction. If your child were training in a sport, too much time on the field might look like disturbed eating and sleeping patterns off the field. If your child spends so long curled up in a corner reading every day they forget to shower or do their homework, you might be concerned they have a reading addiction. All hobbies, interests, and responsibilities should be carried out in moderation.

The concern should not be so much about the amount your child plays video games, but about how much they are accomplishing in the real world when they are *not* playing. If you feel your child sacrifices important facets of their life like a full-night's sleep to play games, you might set limits on their gaming hours. If your child plays video games four hours per day and still does their chores, completes homework, participates with family, there is likely nothing to worry about. Regardless, the appropriate amount of time spent on video games should be established within the family ahead of time and adjusted accordingly, not preemptively.

Playing video games might be helpful for increasing your child's critical thinking but detrimental to their chore schedule. If the goals are not met, maybe video game time gets cut back while you focus on developing personal responsibility together. If the goals are accomplished well, maybe extra time gets added. Every family is going to do it a little differently: there is no prescription for a healthy three hours of video games per night. Maturity, time management, and personal responsibility are all contributions to determine how much game time is healthy for your child.

MONITORING CONTENT BY AGE GROUP

Part of growing up means demonstrating certain levels of responsibility to unlock new benefits, like an extended curfew, time home-alone, or watching an R-rated movie. Likewise, children should demonstrate maturity to handle games with mature content. Games rated for everyone ten-years old and older (E10+) should not magically unlock the day your son or daughter turns ten. Instead, they should work to prove they have mastered maturity for the concepts that caused the game to have a higher rating. If your child wants to play *Crash Bandicoot*, can they show they are mature enough not to slap their siblings with Crash's signature spin attack? I have seen nine-year-old clients show more maturity than the seventeen-year-olds who come in hoping to play NC-17 games with me. Age does not equate to maturity, and maturity is a necessary skill to maintain a healthy relationship with video games.

Contrary to popular belief, the collection of mental health, socialization, and explicit content troubles commonly associated with video games are not prevalent enough for most parents to worry about. So long as your child is a fully-functioning member of your family, their video game hobby is likely just that: a hobby.

VIDEO GAMES: OUR HERO!

If there was ever a time in history that demonstrated the cultural significance of video games, it was during the COVID-19 pandemic. Careers shifted from cubicle to kitchen tables. Sport and show arenas shut their doors for the unforeseeable future. Friends and family had to greet each other through windows, whether digital or glass. Locked down and lonely, the majority of society had lost their socialization options. Restrictions put in place to help curb the pandemic left us looking for a place to socialize without putting anyone at risk. Video games heard our collective call and came to our rescue. Video Games were even recognized by the World Health Organization (WHO) as an important way to stay connected to friends, family, and social relationships during this time.

Different games helped people cope with the pandemic lockdowns in unique ways, but there were three games or game collections most credited for keeping people sane during this strange, isolating time.

1. ANIMAL CROSSING: NEW HORIZONS

The fifth addition to the *Animal Crossing* series was released on the Nintendo Switch just as lockdowns around the world took effect. The game sold five million digital copies in the first month, smashing the world record to pieces. The game became so popular that from March to June, gamers could not find a Switch anywhere, much less the game itself.

In *New Horizons*, the player takes the form of a plump, cartoon boy or girl with customizable features. They move to a remote island to start a new life. The island is essentially a blank slate for players to fill with furniture, attractions, landscapes, and anthropomorphic animal friends who move into little patches of island property. The game is a life simulator, and the players can choose how they want to progress their island on a day-to-day basis. They can fish, catch bugs, water plants, or take a nap with their animal villagers under a shady tree. The relaxing, fully customizable, creativity sandbox that is *New Horizons* became a safe haven for gamers looking for an escape while they wait for the world to open up again.[8]

Not only did players of *New Horizons* find an escape from the humdrum world passing by outside isolation, they also found a safe place to interact with other people. The addition of the island airport allows players to invite friends to their island. Players

---

[8] Zhu, Lin. *The Psychology behind Video Games during COVID-19 Pandemic: A Case Study of Animal Crossing: New Horizons*. Wiley Periodicals LLC. Accessed November 22, 2021. https://onlinelibrary.wiley.com/doi/10.1002/hbe2.221.

communicate through small text bubbles that pop up above their avatars or have their avatar react with cutesy actions like blushing, waving, and dancing. The Nintendo Switch app added support for the game, which opened options like faster typing and a voice chat feature. Discord servers started popping up for trading, visiting, and chatting. A whole community formed during a period of mandatory social distancing.

As lockdown went on, *New Horizons* players started using the wildly customizable game to supplement real outings missing from their day-to-day lives. Some built virtual restaurants and invited their friends. Some turned their island into a giant obstacle course for their friends to navigate. The collection of islands acted as a virtual world through which players could still take part in the activities disallowed by COVID. An in-game update in June 2020 included special wedding items, which led to couples hosting virtual weddings and recreations of ceremonies COVID stole from them in the real world.

While the game did offer a place for players to "meet up" and spend virtual time together, it also served as a form of escapism. The relaxing music, easy progression, and friendly animal faces made the game a much *softer* place to spend time than the panicked, restricted, real world. Using video games for escapism can be beneficial short term, but as a clinician, I recommend only allowing video games to serve this purpose when other, healthy coping mechanisms are practiced as well.

2. ESPORTS

COVID-19 took a toll on almost every industry on the planet, and the world of sports was no exception. Traditional sports leagues were faced with hard questions following the 2020 season cancellations: how do we keep playing sports in a world with no close contact? How do fans safely attend a game with stadium seats?

They had to get creative, not just to maintain connections with fans, but to save professional sports altogether.

Professional league sports rely on broadcasting as one of three main sources of income. Major League Baseball had a $5 billion contract to deliver broadcast media in 2020. The NBA had a $24 billion TV deal in place. An unexpected shutdown with no deadline threatened to put major league sports out of business for good.

With no possible outlet for real-live sports, the major leagues turned to video games.9 The NBA started a 2K competition and allowed sports networks to broadcast the players to audiences as if they were watching a live-action basketball tournament. ESPN and Fox Sports broadcasted esports competitions on live TV. NASCAR drivers got behind the wheel and raced on a virtual track with a digital platform called iRacing and FS1 broadcasted the whole race, right down to the pre-race National Anthem.10

Video games saved the world of sports by providing major leagues with an alternative to broadcast to fans at home. Major leagues got to keep their income flowing and sports networks kept fans engaged with the world of sports—even if it looked a little different for a while.

3. *AMONG US*

Among Us was first released in 2018, but it was not met with success. However, once COVID-19 struck, 85 million players hopped on the spaceship from March-September 2020 as gamers around the world scoured the Steam game store for games they could play in groups.

---

[9] Brambilla Hall, Stefan. "This Is How COVID-19 Is Affecting the World of Sports." World Economic Forum, April 9, 2020. https://www.weforum.org/agenda/2020/04/sports-covid19-coronavirus-excersise-specators-media-coverage/

[10] Baker, Kendall. "NASCAR Leads the Virtual Sports Charge amid Coronavirus Outbreak." Axios, March 23, 2020. https://www.axios.com/coronavirus-virtual-sports-nascar-video-games-a25392ae-8ee6-4739-bdc3-2514b85562dd.html.

Among Us is an online multiplayer "Who Dunnit" like the schoolyard game Mafia. In *Among Us*, up to ten players are crew members on a spaceship. Eight players are astronauts trying to complete space tasks, but one player is an imposter who breaks the ship and kills the crew. The goal of the game is to vote out the imposter before they kill you, or to finish the day's tasks before the whole crew dies. If you are the imposter, your goal is to methodically kill off each player while escaping detection. Since the world's youth could not get together and play card games together on the couch, they found *Among Us* and decided it was the next best option.

Among Us gained popularity during COVID because it was highly social: kids could not go to the park or get some dinner together after a day of virtual school, but they could interact with each other through this cooperative game. One of the biggest draws of *Among Us* was how simple the gameplay felt: it was a catalyst for conversation, but not distracting enough to take away from any bonding happening between players in the game's chat feature. Through a game based on sneaking around, accusing other players, and surviving in a high-stress environment, *Among Us* ended up acting as a therapeutic safe space for players to confide in each other and connect.

The lockdown during the COVID-19 pandemic helped show how valuable video games can be: they provided an alternative to in-person socialization and prevented us from feeling the harshest effects of isolation. This alternative form of communication has a caveat—it cannot act as a long-term solution for lack of social interaction. When we are not locked down all the time, we do not need video games as our only option for communication. Online community gatherings and gameplay can be useful and should not be ruled out, as long as they are considered one way to socialize among many.

BENEFITS OF VIDEO GAMES FOR OUR CHILDREN

Video games are not as horrible for our children as they are made out to be. In fact, video games can be beneficial for them. Developing minds can use video games to develop critical thinking and problem-solving skills, like my son learns while he plays *Pokémon*. They can also promote self-exploration and personal growth.

When our children play a role-playing game (RPG), they can become deeply immersed in the role of the hero. They are directing this hero, making choices from the hero's perspective, and participating in the hero's mythology. Reading *Robin Hood* might resonate with some children with strong imaginations and attention spans, and video game players can project attributes onto characters and their mythos in video games.

The basic, silent hero in video games like *The Legend of Zelda* gives the hero life, but actions chosen by the player give the hero's life meaning. The game's story requires choices, and those choices create a narrative for the player's avatar, which may represent internal manifestations of the player's personality. They then have the freedom to explore the game's mythos as an idealized manifestation of themselves. Your child might not be in a position to leave home and explore the ruins of an ancient civilization, but they can explore the same experience in a simulated setting and adapt to challenges and insights along the way. Self-exploration through the lens of a video game avatar further enhances children's experiences and understanding of real world problems, solutions, and strategies for handling difficult situations.

Of course, RPGs are not the only video games available. Games with more narrative structures like *The Last of Us* can help children with self-exploration, but straightforward person vs. person (PvP) games like *Mortal Kombat* can provide different benefits like stimulation and catharsis. There is nothing more relaxing than pounding a green ninja into the ground after a long day! Clinicians who use geek culture to connect with their clients have not worked with a single client using one type of game. Clients interested in video games for therapeutic use try different perspectives and play styles to experience the multitude of benefits video games offer. If one client likes Mortal Kombat, we introduce them to side-scrollers like Mega Man to encourage problem-solving skills. Sometimes loud, bright, short games like these are most interesting to children when they are not experiencing enough stimulation at home or in school. Clinicians make a constellation out of their observation and ask the client if something is missing in their life; maybe their homework is too easy or they have nothing to do after school. Then, we discuss how to rework their environment to include more stimulation. By exploring multiple types of video games, we can better understand our clients' wants and needs. The new understanding can improve and personalize a therapeutic personal care plan, the same way it can improve a parenting approach.

START ENGAGING

So how do you start engaging in video games with your child?

You start by getting your ass kicked.

If you are new to gaming, your child will probably defeat you in every title on the market, besting you in duels, races, or puzzles while you fumble to learn the controls, but that is okay. It is healthy to give our children the chance to be experts. It makes them feel like they matter and their interests matter to you. Let them show you the special kick combo or the hidden cave on the other end of the map. They will be so excited to teach you a new trick they will not mind how terrible you are at controlling your avatar at first.

Nintendo Switch games (*The Legend of Zelda, Animal Crossing, Super Mario Odyssey*) are the most family-friendly games available. They are also extremely collaborative and most of them feature multiplayer options where the players split controls. I use *Super Mario Odyssey* with my clients. I control Mario and my client controls his hat — which also controls the camera. When we play together, I tell them, "I'm going to move over here and you have to keep up with me." We work on their communication and collaboration skills. If they do not communicate well enough, I wander off. This method focuses clients and forces them to take control and give constructive direction to me. When we are finished, we take a moment to look at what communication styles were constructive and which could be handled a little better next time.

When parents participate in multiplayer games with their kids or split up gameplay to complete a narrative single-player game together, they bond with their kids and take an active role in their learning experience. Parents get to witness firsthand how beneficial video games can be, and children can feel empowered by their parents' active role in their interests.

TRICKS AND TIPS TO USE ALONG THE WAY

While we are learning how to finally beat our child in *Super Smash Brothers*, we can take a few practical steps to prevent them from experiencing too much of the online world before we are able to catch up and supervise. Here are a few tools to take with you while you learn about video games:

- **Parental Controls:** These controls add an extra layer of protection to video games with online access. They can be set to block access completely or ping your phone for approval or denial. These controls can be set up in the console's settings.

- **Financial Locks:** These locks prevent in-game or in-app purchases, which can be made completely on accident if the player is not paying enough attention to the subtle paywalls. This is a great tool to protect your wallet while your child explores a new game before he understands financial responsibility. These can usually be found in a setting on your phone, console, within the app itself.

- **ESRB Ratings:** Entertainment Software Rating Board (ESRB) ratings helps parents gain preliminary knowledge of a game's suitability for their child. The ESRB divides their ratings into three sections: Rating Categories, Content Descriptions, and Interactive Elements. Each section gives details about age appropriateness and content of interest for parents. Every video game lists its ESRB rating on the back of its box. Digital purchases will display the rating on the order screen.

My monomyth began with a deep love of video games and brought me to the creation of Geek Therapy and eventually Geek Therapeutics. The benefits video games have to offer both children and adults are bound only by the player's imagination. Once we let go of the misconception of video games themselves being a danger, we open up a whole new universe to explore with our children.

CHAPTER 4

DUNGEONS & DRAGONS

"It's not just a kid's game. It's a manual."
— Dustin, Stranger Things

After the Unholy Wars decimated our world, survivors struggled to settle in the remnants. The most powerful survivors formed factions and used strong magicks to stake their claim on the cities. The cunning took to the forests, the brave locked in never-ending battles, and the rest of us strive for survival.

You scrape by as a Hero-for-Hire, taking side work from people too powerful or too weak for questing. Your most recent venture completed, you head to a nearby village for new jobs. You see a sign for The Whimpering Wyvern hanging by a single, rusty hook before a dilapidated shack. Two orcs stumble out the swinging door with empty mugs.

Inside the dingy tavern, you spot a few stragglers clinging to rusty bar stools in the low light. A slab of pine crudely nailed to the back wall functions as the Job Board. Upon the Board hangs a parcel with a single pull tab dangling from the bottom. You step over an unconscious halfling on your way toward the Job Board and notice a gaggle of adventure-looking types in one of the hovel's only booths. They each have a pull tab in hand.

Roll for Initiative.

Before video games, monologues like this introduced gamers to new, fantastical journeys. Without controllers to move their avatars, screens to view their environments, or sound effects to bring their actions to life, gamers commanded their heroic characters by making choices in a story. This form of gaming is called a role-playing game (RPG). In 1974, this immersive, imaginative, collaborative game type revolutionized the world of gaming with the popularization of *Dungeons & Dragons* (D&D).

INTRODUCTION: THE BIRTH OF A CAMPAIGN

Role-playing games are characterized by their storytelling, with a plethora of storylines for players to complete to obtain in-game gear, abilities, and reputations. There are a variety of popular tabletop roleplaying games (TTRPGs) titles your child might love including *Warhammer* and *Call of Cthulhu*, but we will examine the genre by focusing on D&D. The concepts we cover can be easily applied to all RPGs. TTRPGs like D&D use unique character builds, chance mechanics like dice rolls, and storytelling in make-believe worlds to determine the direction of their **campaigns**. A campaign is the continuous storyline or set of adventures within the game. A D&D campaign requires at least two players, taking on the roles defined below:

Game Master: The GM (or Dungeon Master, DM) acts as both the author and the narrator for the game's overarching story. They use D&D guidebooks to choose different styles, settings, and stories from an existing collection, or customize their own campaign using well-known D&D elements, world mythologies, and other storytelling scenarios. For example, a GM could narrate the popular *Storm King's Thunder* storyline, in which players fight against giant clans in a wintry mountain region, build a campaign around the Greek Labyrinth to defeat Minotaur, or even guide adventurers to battle a team of supervillains from well-known comic series.

The GM determines the general plot structure, but they must have strong improvisation skills too as the players' choices ultimately dictate the campaign's direction.

Non-Playable Characters: The GM also takes on the role of non-playable characters, or NPCs. These imaginary characters fill out the fictional world around the players. In terms of the Hero's Journey, NPCs can act as threshold guardians, tricksters, mentors, or enemies. The more depth NPCs have, the more enjoyable the game becomes for the players.

Playable Characters: One or more players other than the GM create playable characters (PCs) to navigate the GM's world. Each player defines their character with a combination of fighting class, fantasy race, equipment, attributes, and personality. In the world of D&D, the PCs are often referred to as "adventurers."

Every character creation choice yields strengths *and* weaknesses. The rogue may be dexterous enough to pickpocket enemies, but is rarely strong enough to defeat them alone. The barbarian might be strong enough to take on three foes at once, but is not intelligent enough to craft healing potions for their wounds. The wizard may be intelligent enough to cast complex spells, but lacks the stamina to scale castle walls. No character can be built to master everything, requiring collaboration, companionship, communication, and clever thinking for players to overcome obstacles in the storyline.

In our opening monologue, the GM asks the player to choose their character's next action. The player's choice is motivated by their character's unique build. After choosing an action, the player must roll dice to determine their odds of a successful outcome. A character built for stealth will have a better chance of eavesdropping on other adventurers than one built to fight. A bard who loves performing would be less likely to adventure alone and ignore a potentially captive audience. No character can succeed every time they act, but players can consider characters' strengths and weaknesses to improve their chances of accomplishing their goals.

Players in a D&D campaign are responsible for **role-playing** as their characters. Role-playing varies based on the players' comfort level. Some groups of players may enjoy dressing up as their characters. Some GMs might adopt a new voice to represent each unique NPC. Those less familiar or comfortable with role-play might prefer to say "I stab with my enchanted scabbard" in their own voice and clothes.

DEMAND & DOORWAYS

The original versions of D&D used classic TTRPG elements like pen-and-paper character sheets, heavy sets of dice, and maps drawn on hexagonal grids, but digitization has helped D&D reach a wider audience. Online versions of D&D like *Roll20* allow players to digitally store their character sheets, reference the campaigns' rules and elements with a click, and roll virtual dice that automatically calculate the outcomes of every action.

Platforms like *Roll20* and *Foundry* can be helpful for parents and children diving into the D&D world for the first time. Online services allow new players to explore D&D without investing in physical versions, and the built-in glossaries are great for quick answers as beginners learn the D&D mythology.

Other doorways into the world of D&D started cropping up in popular culture in the late 2010s. There are dozens of podcasts where comedians, voice actors, and other D&D enthusiasts get together and play through a campaign to entertain an audience. Shows like *Dimension 20* and *Dungeons & Daddies* provide exciting stories to their listeners while demonstrating the game's flow and rules.

The D&D content creators of *Critical Role* published their first live-recorded episode in March 2015, their 100th episode in June 2017, and became the top-grossing channel on live-streaming platform Twitch.tv by 2020. The cast is a group of friends who have careers as voice actors outside of *Critical Role*. Each episode of *Critical Role* is around four hours in length and is broadcasted on a weekly basis on Twitch.tv/criticalrole. Tens of thousands of viewers watch the livestream every week, and the recorded episodes published on YouTube have hundreds of thousands of views each.

D&D shows up in popular culture in other ways, too. Shows like T*he Simpsons, Futurama, South Park*, and *Adventure Time* have all featured episodes based on D&D. In Netflix's hit series *Stranger Things*, characters play D&D in scenes together, while the plot of each season operates on the framework of a D&D campaign. These shows' references to D&D both acknowledge and bolster TTRPGs' place in pop culture canon.

So, if D&D is so popular, accessible, and fun, why would we be concerned when our kids play?

DEVILS & DEVIANTS

Parents are not thrilled about the idea of their children sitting in dark basements, huddled around heroic and demonic figurines for hours on end. If they peek in on their kids' session, they might be horrified when they hear comments like, "I set the building on fire so they can't get out," or "I loot all the corpses." This kind of behavior would be abhorrent if acted out in the real world. Some parents worry if they allow their kids to play D&D, they are encouraging their kids to act like bloodlusting crusaders. D&D was surrounded by anxiety after its debut and is one of the most well-known examples of a moral panic from recent history. It was dubbed the Satanic Panic, and it arose in the 1980s as parents, politicians, and parishioners espoused conspiracies about Satanic worship taking place in secret, and many pointed fingers at D&D. In 1985, psychiatrist Thomas Radecki and anti-occult activist Patricia Pulling formed B.A.D.D. (Bothered About Dungeons & Dragons). These two believed D&D was a gateway into the world of the occult for children. B.A.D.D. representatives gave speeches across the country, making claims about the evil lurking within the game.

Many parents heeded the speeches from B.A.D.D. and feared Dungeons & Dragons would expose their kids to real-world evil and tempt them to act out. Pastor Jon Quigley of Lakeview Full Gospel Fellowship claimed, "the game is an occult tool that opens up young people to influence or possession by demons." Many schools, clubs, and organizations banned D&D outright, despite the lack of reputable evidence to prove the game had an adverse effect on children.

D&D's reputation never fully recovered from the Satanic Panic, but today we have better research. Dozens of high-quality studies have shown the benefits of TTRPGs on developing minds, particularly when the GM is familiar with the game's rules and its therapeutic potential.

Wayne D. Blackmon, M.D. documented cases of psychotherapeutic treatment enabled a patients' experience with ongoing games of D&D. In these cases, role playing serves as a safe space for his patients to explore their emotions, work with those feelings, and eventually gain mastery over problematic moods.

Dr. Blackmon discovered role-play can reveal actual characteristics of the players. This means troubling traits can be exacerbated by the game, but a trained GM and therapist can use the waking fantasy to help patients identify emotions, work through issues, and build self-efficacy. Say a player revealed their temper during a frustrating conversation with an NPC. The GM can help the player explore different ways to approach their temper through the NPC's response. The NPC could refuse to help the player's character, leaving them stuck on in the middle of their quest. Then, the GM might discuss how the player could apologize to the NPC and patch up the relationship. This allows the player to explore and improve their own characteristics in a make-believe, low-consequence environment.

Geek Therapeutics brought D&D to Texas Christian University (TCU) and introduced some of their students to the game. Religion was at the center of the Satanic Panic and followers of religion are usually the most wary about engaging in D&D. We were diligent about addressing any concerns raised by staff, students, and parents. We discussed the experience of playing and how D&D serves to benefit its participants. Our open communication allowed us to bridge the gap between the students at TCU and D&D's traditional fanbase, and the students learned valuable lessons, even from introductory gameplay. When I checked in on the university's students several years after introducing them to the game, I was delighted to hear the school decided to maintain an after school D&D program. In fact, the program's demand grew so large that they now run five groups per week. The students in the D&D program are some of the highest ranking students at the university, and their performance is believed to be a direct result of their time playing D&D together.

Kids do not play D&D with the hopes they will learn how to join the occult. They play because the game is interesting and engaging. People can role-play as powerful versions of themselves. They can explore different personality traits and what it might be like to take them on.

DECISIONS & DEPRAVITY

Like video games, D&D allows players to take on the role of the hero and become powerful enough to defeat strong, formidable foes. D&D takes the player's choice even further than most video games by letting the player become a villain.

Characters are built with **alignments**, which explain their morality and personal attitudes toward society and order. Many GMs do not allow their players to play characters with Evil alignments. They are concerned evil actions from one party member might ruin gameplay for the other players. When I GM, I let my players choose any alignment they want, but it becomes my responsibility to rein them in when they make nefarious choices.

Players who make evil choices must experience consequences for their actions. If an evil character decides to steal from a hero, they might be arrested and have to spend time in jail. If they kill an NPC or another player without justification, they might become a target themselves. Either way, they risk upsetting other players. Emotional and physical consequences trigger character growth when the character (and the player) is forced to reconcile with their choices. That growth can spark an entire transformation.

When our clients play D&D, we see the transformation within them. We worked with a kid, Billy, with severe ADHD and impulse control behaviors issues. We started him off in a group for D&D. During the first session, Billy kept interrupting other players.

"You're not playing that character right," he moaned, trying to usurp power from the GM, "You can't make that NPC chaotic evil, the game doesn't allow you to do that."

He kept reaching across the table to snag dice from other players. He argued with the GM about minute details in the setting, plot, and different rules. Billy's impulsive behavior and disruptions derailed the GM several times, interrupting the flow of the game for the other players. We had to step in to prevent the situation from escalating.

"Hey, we appreciate the information and we're going to take it under consideration," we responded without shaming him or trying to stop him. "We've designed this campaign differently, so we're going to play it this way. It's okay if it breaks the rules a little."

Rather than shut down his more impulsive actions, we allowed them to play out. We did the same when it came to in-game impulses.

"I don't like this person," Billy would say. "I'm going to push them down the well."

"Okay," We would respond, "but remember there's always consequences for our behaviors." The GM also prompted the other players, saying, "How does the group feel about this action, does anyone wish to intervene?" The GM provided options for the other players to help them grow as well.

When Billy's character pushed the person, he started a full-on brawl in a peaceful part of town and landed in the town's jail. We used it as an opportunity to reflect on his actions.

"Oh man, you got locked up in jail," I told Billy. "Now the rest of the crew has to jailbreak you. What is that like for the group to have to stop their quest and go break your character out of jail, because they made a behavior move that was not appreciated by other people?"

We had group discussions about how Billy's actions affected the rest of the party.

"You know," the other players said, "it really took away from what we could have been doing instead. We could have been making progress toward discovering why there is magical energy coming from the mountain."

Billy retreated, feeling shameful, and told them to leave him in jail if their quest was so important. At this point, it was time for an intervention. It was time for the group to rally behind him and show him how important he was to them.

"You're part of the group, so what happens with you also happens with us," they said. "We're not going to leave you behind, man. We're not going to let you separate yourself. We don't split the group."

Overall, the sessions produced amazing, touching, emotional moments between the players. The kids felt a sense of community and pride in their accomplishments together. Billy stopped interrupting the game and using his character to push NPCs. By the tenth session, he was a fully-engaged and valuable member of the party.

Billy's story is one of many in which kids use D&D as an opportunity to grow through their characters. Billy was introduced to the negative consequences of his character's negative actions when he upset the party. He also realized positive consequences when he worked together with his party to complete the campaign. The non-scripted nature of the game allowed him to express himself naturally as he would in real life and he learned the natural outcomes. Under the supervision of a therapist, he was able to develop new ways to interact with others to benefit both his D&D character and his impulse control. Your child might not have ADHD or impulsive behaviors like Billy, but you can analyze patterns in their RPG experiences to help them hone their real-life character.

DEVELOPMENT & DISCUSSION

Dr. Blackmon's research and my own experiences suggest RPG characters can provide insights about the players behind them. Further, we can use the RPG environment therapeutically to help our children grow. An understanding of psychosocial development theory helps parents identify which concepts our children might be developing and how D&D can intersect with them. The two psychosocial development stages most applicable to Dungeons & Dragons gameplay are stage four, Industry versus Inferiority (ages 6-11), and stage five, Identity versus Role Confusion (ages 10-20).

According to psychosocial development theory, children ages six to eleven are commonly in the Industry vs. Inferiority stage, meaning they are discovering their potential to be good and bad at different tasks. They feel good accomplishing tasks they excel at, and feel bad when they are unable to succeed in other areas. Internalizing their successes can lead to an industrious, go-getting attitude whereas failures can manifest a sense of inferiority. D&D is a great place for children to explore these feelings because no character can master every skill. Each one has its own share of strengths and weaknesses.

Role-playing as a hero in D&D, children can feel strong, capable, and resilient, using their strengths to overcome challenges. Players are excited to upgrade their characters, learn new skills, and conquer formidable foes. As the player experiences success in D&D, they can bolster their self-image as industrious rather than inferior, encouraging them to continue to take risks and attempt new skills within and without the game.

When your child inevitably comes across a challenge their character cannot overcome because of a weakness, they can learn to cope with inferiority and practice creative problem-solving. They could ask for help from a teammate and discover all the benefits being in a party has to offer, or they could develop new ways to succeed in areas they would otherwise find challenging.

For example, if your child gets nervous meeting new people or presenting in front of the class, you might encourage them to rehearse social interactions in the low-consequence environment of a TTRPG. Perhaps you craft a gameplay situation that requires your child to give a rousing speech to fill their companions with courage before the big battle. Among a small group of trusted gamers, your child can test their performance in a social situation outside of their usual comfort zone. If they succeed and fill the characters' hearts with courage, they might bolster their public speaking skills in general. If they fail to muster up a powerful speech, they are in a safe space to try again with a different approach. Either way, D&D provides fun opportunities to explore individual strengths and weaknesses for personal development.

If we summarize stage four as the stage in which children discover the world, the fifth stage is where they discover their place in it. The fifth stage, Identity versus Role Confusion, mostly occurs between ages ten through twenty. When a child develops their Identity, they gain a stronger sense of who they are. This can play out as learning what careers would be satisfying for them, or how they identify sexually. Role Confusion is when a child senses they are performing a role out of alignment with who they are. This could be a child who wants to be a star athlete at school but has to drop the football team to help out at home. Or it could be the child who values their independence, but is stuck feeling subordinate in their personal relationships. We can use D&D to help children explore their identities and fulfill meaningful roles by evaluating how they create their characters.

Playing a support-role character can help a player uncover their desire to pursue a nursing career, while role-playing as a different genders can help a player explore their sexual and gender identities. Playing characters of different fictional races can help characters understand their own racial identity and how to accept the identities of those with unfamiliar backgrounds. When we notice our child consistently playing as a furtive assassin class who moves in the shadows, we might ask if they prefer work behind the scenes in real life, or if they see themselves as someone who does not need much attention to be happy. If our child is attracted to a character with an engineering class who solves problems with brains over brawn, we might ask if they find intelligence highly valuable, or if they wish they were better at math and science in the classroom. Players can explore different roles by tinkering with the races, classes, and attributes of their character builds to better comprehend who they are and how they see themselves in the world.

We can further evaluate identity through one of D&D's most well-known artifacts: the Character Alignment Chart. This chart has become a meme and is applied to characters outside the world of D&D, inanimate objects, and other recognizable parts of everyday life. For example, the chart below includes an example based on types of coffee.

D&D Character Alignment Chart

| Lawful Good
Acts with duty and honor, follows all laws
Latte | Neutral Good
Believes in the greater good, breaks some laws to achieve it
Iced coffee | Chaotic Good
Does whatever it takes to achieve the greater good, often with disorganized plans
Frappuccino |
| --- | --- | --- |
| Lawful Neutral
Follows personal code dutifully
Espresso | True Neutral
Acts in favor of personal interests, unaligned with right or wrong
Black coffee | Chaotic Neutral
Abandons all rules in favor of personal desires
Red eye |
| Lawful Evil
Follows strict codes and laws in favor of evil
Irish coffee | Neutral Evil
Acts without order or passion, follows personal code
Instant coffee | Chaotic Evil
No respect for laws or others, pursues chaos for chaos' sake and often destroys for fun
Redbull |

Alignments are a combination of two factors: morality and willingness to abide by societal rules. A chaotic good character disregards the laws, but always tries to fight for the greater good, even if their end goal hurts others. Robin Hood's habit of robbing the rich to feed the poor is a popular example of a chaotic good character. A lawful evil character is the opposite: they follow laws to a T, but enjoy hurting others to get ahead. Crossroad demons, or characters who make dangerous deals with desperate people, fall under the lawful evil alignment.

We can apply the alignment chart to the real world to help us understand our children's sense of morality and place in society. If your child chooses to play a chaotic good character, they might have good intentions, but feel too restricted by rules to accomplish their goals. We can observe players' character creation choices to understand how they view the world and how they prefer to navigate it.

DISCOURSE & DISCIPLINE

D&D is an extremely beneficial pastime for our growing children when parents understand the best ways to engage with the game and our kids. Diving into a complex fantasy world with so many choices can seem overwhelming for many parents, but there are plenty of resources to help newcomers understand the flow of a well-organized campaign.

Listening to D&D podcasts or watching live streams of campaigns are some of the best ways to learn the game without picking up heavy rulebooks. The only moments missing from these TTRPG sessions are when players take too long to calculate their dice roll total or when they take snack breaks. Brennan Lee Mulligan, GM for *Dimension 20's* D&D campaign *Fantasy High*, told his viewers,

"If you've watched season one of *Fantasy High*, you can DM." Listening to D&D sessions can help build an understanding of the game's natural flow and how good DMs demonstrate flexibility when presented with tricky situations from their players.

If listening to well-versed players move through campaigns with enviable ease does not make you comfortable enough to start a game with your expert child, you can always visit your local friendly game shop and see if they hold D&D nights. This route also allows you to participate in a party alongside your child without either of you playing the GM role. Most local game shops are not merely accepting of new players, they are excited to welcome you into their world!

A deeply-engrossing world of self-exploration can lead to hours of play, pulling people away from a more balanced life. To counter this, most D&D groups dedicate one night a week to their sessions and cut off their games around the two-hour mark. Setting a time limit like this for your child can give them time to engage in D&D without letting it detract from real-world responsibilities.

Playing D&D can be initially difficult because of its learning curve, but as long as you are willing to learn, be imaginative, and stay curious, you will be conquering new lands in no time. Then, you can use your new familiarity with the game to apply its most common concepts to your child's life.

The endless possibilities of D&D can also be problematic, as children can paint their experiences with unsavory decision-making. Players are able to be racist, sexist, or needlessly violent in the world of D&D, which ought to be discouraged by the GM through fitting in-game consequences. Many D&D sessions in modern play begin with a "Session Zero," which should include the group going over consent factors. Here, players can discuss topics to leave out of the campaign, like violence, death, romance, or any other element they are uncomfortable role-playing.

Another way to mitigate unchecked problematic behaviors is to be present in your child's D&D campaigns to ensure characters are treated fairly and rude choices receive fitting consequences. It is impossible to be there for every session to monitor the judgments of your child's in-game actions, but parents are not supposed to be helicopters over their children's shoulders. The most parents can do is teach their kids the consequences of their actions and encourage them to make healthy choices when they are on their own.

GAMEPLAY: THE THREE PILLARS

If you want to guide your child's role-playing experience as a competent GM, there are three pillars of gameplay you should attend to: exploration, social interaction, and combat. When the three pillars are well-balanced, you can craft the most enjoyable games.

Exploration: This pillar refers to characters' interaction with the world throughout the campaign. Good exploration means players can discover hidden clues and treasures, venture down branching paths, and learn about the history and culture of the fantasy world. GMs can help players feel connected to the world through maps and other props that represent the environment they explore.

Social interaction: The depth of interaction between NPCs and PCs is known as social interaction. GMs can bolster this pillar by including a dialogue-rich NPC as an early ally, or by writing deep backstories to flesh out NPCs' likes, dislikes, and attitudes. They can also include puzzles in dungeons that require intimate knowledge of each other's backstories to solve, encouraging the characters to get to know each other and form a bond.

Combat: In D&D, combat is in a turn-based event that combines PC builds, NPC builds, the environment, and dice rolls to determine outcomes. Vivid descriptions of enemies and their environments help players feel connected to their choices in combat. For example, the GM might strengthen this pillar by mentioning a precarious chandelier in the foyer so players can choose to drop on their foes. Or, they could color a highway robber as weak and nervous, clueing in players to the possibility of peaceful resolution instead of a violent one. A wide range of options can discourage repetitive fights and encourage creative solutions.

When we custom build quests around an individual's struggles, they are free to explore hardships in a more comfortable setting. If a client is struggling with grief, we can build a campaign to explore their character's quest to scatter a loved one's ashes, like the video game *God of War*. If they are experiencing anxiety in social situations, we can promote interactions with more NPCs so the player feels like they are succeeding at interacting with multiple people, even though they are only communicating with the GM in different roles. With a degree of separation and an entertaining backdrop, GMs can design D&D campaigns to confront specific issues without making the players feel too uncomfortable.

SPELL SHEETS

Parents can use D&D's spell system with their children to communicate energy levels. Magic-wielding D&D characters only get a certain number of spell slots per day on their character sheets. Some character sheets have cantrips, which are spells and actions performed without burning a spell slot. Every character has a different number of maximum spells per day based on their build. We can use cantrips multiple times in a day, but spells can only be used so many times before we have to rest. Harder, more demanding tasks require more spell slots to complete. Similarly, every child has an amount of energy to exert on physical or emotional tasks in a day.

Discuss with your child which daily tasks are cantrips, which take one spell slot, and which take three. Tasks like brushing teeth and washing hair might be cantrips for some kids and a spell slot for others. If taking out the trash and doing the dishes both use up two spell spots, we probably do not want to do them both on the same day.

When a child says, "I'm low on spell slots" or "I'm out of spell slots," it is an engaging way for them to express they are out of energy and need a long rest (eight hours in D&D) to reset their energy levels and reopen spell slots. Parents can use this code too when it is time for bed and they do not have any more spell slots to play another game of cards. As the older, higher level wizard in your house, you might have more spell slots than your child, but some of your tasks are valued higher. Driving to work might take three points and working for eight hours might take more. When a code like this exists between parents and children, it allows everyone to express their emotions through a comforting lens, providing a better understanding of internal states.

Spell sheets are one of the dozens of TTRPG artifacts we can use to benefit our children and demonstrate how games like D&D can promote positive interactions with others, personal growth, and creative problem-solving skills.

CHAPTER 5

MAGIC: THE GATHERING & OTHER TCGS

*"Good strategists seize opportunities.
Great strategists make their own."*
— Shelter card, Magic: The Gathering

It seems like most parents understand the benefits of competitive, strategy games in developing children, but they draw the line at fantasy card games. Once winged creatures and magic spells enter the game, parents grow wary of their children focusing too heavily on the fantasy side and not enough on the strategic path to victory.

Children who grow up participating in chess competitions are deemed geniuses by the parenting world, but those who stand victorious at the end of a three-hour game of Elder Highlander Commander (EDH or "Commander") are deemed egomaniacal nerds. Why is there such a stark difference in our approach to traditional trading card games (TCGs) when they take the same amount of skill (if not more) to play as other tabletop card games or chess?

BASIC CARD GAMES

Parents love to play card games with their children, like *Crazy Eights, Uno,* or *Go Fish!*. Basic card games have a multitude of mental benefits: neural plasticity, memory vitality, risk analysis, stress release, and more.[11] Card games are particularly useful in a therapeutic setting due to their accessibility and customization. Fifty-two-card decks are versatile enough to create thousands of games limited only by our imaginations.

The card game *War* might seem boring as the higher of two random cards always wins and there is no strategy, but we can use our imaginations to see the cards as soldiers going head-to-head on the battlefield. *Go Fish!* is similarly simplistic, but a childhood favorite as kids love to imagine "fishing" for cards. Parents might make the game more entertaining by adding sound effects or a "pond" from which players pull their fish.

These games are wonderful because they are easy to play on the surface, but have boundless potential to be adapted for more strategy, fantasy, creativity, and storytelling.

TRADING CARDS & TRADING CARD GAMES (TCGS)

Some card decks exist solely for collection and trading, like Topps baseball and basketball cards. While these cards have no intended mechanics for gameplay, collectors are drawn in by the exciting graphics, statistics, or rarities. Like the standard fifty-two-card French playing card deck, trading cards have the variety and flexibility to allow collectors to use them for new games imagined out of thin air.

In 1993, Wizards of the Coast designed the first trading cards for competitive gaming with the release of *Magic: The Gathering* (MTG, or *Magic*). To this day, *Magic* is the most common TCG with the largest international community of players.

---

[11] Wallace, James. "10 Psychological Benefits of Playing Card Games." Psychreg, August 20, 2021. https://www.psychreg.org/psychological-benefits-playing-card-games/.

Magic combines the versatility of a fifty-two-card French deck with complex mechanics that have become standard in most TCGs, like health points, resources to spend on special moves, and the ability to create a custom deck for dueling opponents. It also has a complex, Turing-complete rule system (meaning the data-manipulation mechanics of the game could be used to replicate a Turing machine...aka a computer) with tens of thousands of card options. Parents might be familiar with TCG franchises like *Pokémon* or *YuGiOh*. These TCGs have thriving collecting, trading, and competitive gaming scenes, but going forward, we are going to focus primarily on MTG for our geeks.

Clinical Psychologist Dr. Lucas Theodore (published as Dr. N. L. Harrington, 2013)—who runs a *Magic* gaming group for patients with autism—states MTG is "not just a game, it's a lifestyle."[12] Young MTG enthusiasts can "play" by collecting cards they find interesting because of their rarity, art, flavor text, or ability. Once they are a bit more experienced, they might prefer building decks based on unique strategies to compete against a variety of MTG players. Players have a unique opportunity to compete with people from different cultures, creeds, and age groups in the MTG world.

Magic engages players similarly to D&D through its complex mythology. Each creature, enchantment, and Land has its place among the lore of the MTG multiverse. Players take on the role of Planeswalkers, traversing the multiverse and collecting energy from different planes. That energy is spent summoning powerful monsters to fight for them when they encounter other Planeswalkers.

There are several types of battle play in MTG. The most common types are Standard Draft, Constructed, and EDH or Commander. In a draft, players open new packs of cards and take turns drafting from them before using the cards they draft to build forty-card decks. Con-

---

[12] Lewis Harrington, Natasha. "Positive Magic, Part 1." CoolStuffInc.com, October 14, 2013. https://www.coolstuffinc.com/a/natasha-lewis-harrington-101413-positive-magic-part-1/.

structed play uses decks of at least sixty cards, and players build their customized deck in advance. Commander is a popular format where each player has a 100 card deck with a "Legendary Creature" card as their commander, and each of the other cards has to be unique (with the exception of "Basic Land" cards).

Draft play relies on players' ability to improvise based on the cards revealed at the opening of a new pack. Constructed play allows for more complex strategies since players can repeat cards up to four times and manipulate statistics more to their advantage depending on their strategy. Commander is popular because players can build decks around their favorite characters from the lore. Commander is also great for groups because while any format can technically allow for multiple players, Commander is the easiest format to scale, usually up to six players in one game.

The goal of competitive play is to reduce the opponent's life points to zero, or use special cards to find other winning conditions ("win-cons"), such as putting a certain number of counters on a Legendary Creature card, or raising your life total above a certain amount, or using the infamous "Triskaidekaphobia" card to get other players' life totals to exactly thirteen.

Depending on the cards in your deck, and your role as a Planeswalker, the way in which you "cast spells" (play cards) can tell a story as you duel with your opponent. Will your tribe of elves overrun your opponent's undead zombies? Will your army of goblins win out over the opposing vampires? Will the humans under your protection survive the endless night on Innistrad and outlast the werewolves? The way you play determines the outcome of the story, which gives you endless opportunities to make critical decisions and develop strategic thinking patterns.

Each player's turn has five stages: a Beginning, a Main Phase, Combat, a second Main Phase, and an End Step. Each stage has different elements that must be carried out in a particular order, very much like the order of operations in a math equation. The stages of a turn are the big parenthesis, containing equations inside the greater equation of someone's turn.

During each stage, players cast spells (play cards) to try and manipulate the outcome of each step in the order of operations to their advantage. Spells can help them "Learn" (draw a card, aka a new spell), summon creatures (play creature cards), or do all sorts of other crazy magic (usually in the form of Instant, Sorcery, and Enchantment cards). However, players are limited to the number of spells they can cast based on the amount of Land cards (resource generators) played on the field and the number of cards in their hand.

Like most card games, players draw a card at the beginning of each of their turns (unless there is a card that says otherwise). In Magic, this is called your "Upkeep." It is as if your character has been traversing the lands of the plane(s) you draw your power from, and the cards in your hand are the resources you have access to based on how the mana (magic) is flowing. Some cards will be called Land cards, of which you can play one per turn (unless there is a card that says otherwise). Once land is on the field, you can "tap" it for "mana" (magical power) to cast your spells (play the other cards in your hand). You must be strategic, though, because once you've tapped a Land card for mana, you cannot "untap" it until the beginning of your next turn (unless there is a card that says otherwise… in MTG there is *always* a card that says otherwise).

Each card in a MTG deck has unique features that benefit the player. These features are described in different areas on the cards:

> **Card Title:** Each card has a specific title in the top left corner for easy identification. Players can have up to four cards of the same name in their deck in Draft and Constructed formats, and one card of the same name in their deck in Commander. The exception to this rule is for Basic Land cards, which are unlimited in any deck in any format.

Mana Cost: Players use mana as currency to play spells. Each card that is not a Land card has a "mana cost" listed in the top right corner, which usually comprises of some colored circles (red, white, green, blue, black) to determine how many lands of a specific color must be tapped, and another number that determines how many additional lands of any color must also be tapped. The color of Land cards usually determines the type of strategy your deck has, and therefore the type of story your deck tells. Green "Forest" cards might call on the beasts of the jungle, blue "Island" cards might call on the monsters of the deep blue sea, and red "Mountains" might allow you to cast aggressive, volcanic, firepower spells.

Card Type: Cards in *Magic* are divided by type: Land, Creature, Artifact, Enchantment, Planeswalker, Instant, and Sorcery. The type is dictated in the center left of the card. Each type has different benefits for the player. Land cards generate mana, creature cards represent spells to summon creatures to attack and defend, and enchantments primarily represent lasting spell effects that can benefit the player or hinder their opponent.[13] Instant card types are special: they are the only cards able to be played out of turn as a reaction to an opponent's move.

Set Symbol: The set symbol is in the center ride and its color indicates the card's rarity. The symbol itself represents which expansion set this card originated from, and therefore how it fits into the overall lore of

---

[13] Heffalump. "Introduction to MTG • Beginner's Guide • MTG Arena Zone." MTG Arena Zone, December 4, 2021. https://mtgazone.com/introduction-to-mtg/#6.

the game. This information does not affect competitive play, but it can help players envision the story their deck is telling.

Rules Text: This is the first set of text on every card. It gives a brief description of the card's effect when placed on the battlefield. Further clarification of a card's abilities is sometimes included in parentheses.

Flavor Text: Beneath the rules text, some cards have a quote or descriptor that provides its backstory in the context of *Magic* mythology. This information does not affect competitive gameplay.

Unlike D&D, though, players are not required to role-play a character to participate in the game. There is no GM to provide narrative structure, and the mythology only exists through flavor text and players' preexisting understanding of the lore. MTG's loose narrative structure exists to provide an engaging premise for players. Any player who prefers not to learn the lore can ignore it and still play based on the game's mechanics. (But that is arguably way less fun.)

Players who *do* choose to engage in the mythology get to explore themselves through imaginative play. Adults are not always as open to play as their children, but MTG gives them an opportunity to reconnect with their inner child. MTG is popular with adults and children alike because of the positive emotions invoked through play. Winning a match is exciting. New decks are promising, and opening the package to sort through new cards feels rewarding. Making decisions based on MTG's lore and logic system boosts confidence and enthralls players. More so than basic card games and trading card collections, MTG is focused on lore and interactive play.

MAGIC: THE PREVAILING

Magic: The Gathering was first released in 1993 by gaming company Wizards of the Coast—the same company would acquire D&D four years later. It was the first trading card game, and as of December 2018, has acquired thirty-five million players worldwide. Its success set the standard for all subsequent TCGs, including *Pokémon, Yu-Gi-Oh*, and *Keyforge*.

The introduction of TCGs to the geek community was revolutionary because it welcomed geeks into a competitive space. Like chess, it allowed competitive people to duel with strategy instead of physical prowess. Unlike chess, TCGs cater to geeks' fantasy interests with rich lore, otherworldly artwork, and a customizable set of game pieces. Competitions help us learn and grow as people, and geeks who did not play sports or found board games too boring stimulate their minds with TCGs. Plus, the Turing-complete rule system allows for virtually unlimited competitive strategies, allowing the game to evolve as players lean into certain deck builds and their opponents learn to counter them.

In TCGs, the rarest or most powerful card available does not automatically "win" you the game. Players have to use a combination of cards' stats, abilities, and synergies to defeat their opponents. Similar to RPGs, every deck combination has its own strengths and weaknesses, so even the most popular deck builds can be dismantled by counter strategy. This allows players more agency in their matches and demands attention, flexibility, and engagement from participants. Children who play MTG experience more complex forms of play than basic card games. This more complex play can easily be transcribed to real life events and help them explore how to deal with everyday problems.

Unsurprisingly, MTG took off in the geek world almost immediately. The first *Magic* World Championship in 1994 was capped at

512 participants. Since then, the MTG World Championship occurs (almost) every year with hundreds of smaller competitions and Pro tours in between. On a smaller scale, almost every community's local friendly game shop (LGFS) hosts MTG game nights and contests. In the late 2010s, the game expanded online through PC, Mac, Android, and iOS games. In 2019, MTG entered the arena of esports and awarded a $10 million prize pool to the winners.

Magic's expansive, enthusiastic community welcomes players of all ages. There are many ways to engage with the game and the community, but some parents find so many options for engagement worrisome. MTG can entice young minds a bit more than their parents are comfortable with. Exploring the concerns most parents have about MTG and other TCGs is imperative to conquer the moral panics and discuss benefits.

MAGIC: THE FRIGHTENING

Although *Magic* started out with cards that borrowed character tropes from D&D, Wizards of the Coast quickly backpedaled to avoid the Satanic Panic's backlash during the mid-1980s and early 1990s. From 1995 to 2002, Wizards of the Coast withdrew all cards with references to demons and replaced them with a similar character called a "horror." Fan favorite card "Demonic Tutor" became "Diabolic Tutor." The artwork on the "Unholy Strength" card had a flaming pentagram removed. Wizards of the Coast resumed printing demonic titles and symbols again when Magic was an undeniably successful, stable, Satan-free game.[14]

Games like D&D and *Magic* include demonic characters because they represent the dark side of traditional fantasy.

---

[14] Rosewater, Mark. "Where Have All the Demons Gone?" Magic: The Gathering. Wizards of the Coast, July 5, 2004. https://magic.wizards.com/en/articles/archive/making-magic/where-have-all-demons-gone-2004-07-05.

CHECKPOINTS AND AUTOSAVES

Players' ability to overcome evil creatures or role-play as evil characters helps them explore these concepts in low-consequence settings. While removing demonic concepts from games lowered satanic exposure, it also removed some potential for education on the topic of evil.

While demonic and infernal references made their way back into *Magic*, the game continued to adjust their concepts to remain accessible for the widest audience. *Magic's* website has a list of all banned and restricted cards below their official statement:[15]

> *"Cards whose art, text, name, or combination thereof that are racially or culturally offensive are banned in all formats. This list is a work in progress....There's much more work to be done as we continue to make our games, communities, and company more inclusive. Know that we work every day to be better and that we hear you. We look forward to sharing more of our plans with you as our games and organization evolve."*

Most TCGs occasionally ban or restrict inappropriate cards from official games. For example, *Yu-Gi-Oh* features a list of banned cards in their Parent's Guide, and Japanese-language *Pokémon* cards are occasionally altered to show less-controversial artwork before being printed in English language. In MTG, some cards depicting scantily-clad women were updated with imagery of more practical, combat-ready pieces of armor. By continuously reviewing their game-legal cards, Wizards of the Coast keeps *Magic* as friendly as possible for younger Planeswalkers.

Magic's website also includes a card directory with descriptions for every card ever distributed. Parents can check their child's cards against this database for more information about how it functions and what good or evil implications it might have in-game. If a

---

[15] "The Gathering: Official Site for MTG News, Sets, and Events." MAGIC the Gathering. Wizards of the Coast. Accessed December 8, 2021. https://magic.wizards.com/en.

card makes you uncomfortable, you can always ban it yourself: no single card makes or breaks a player's ability to strategize.

However, you should discuss this new boundary with your child before enacting it so they do not feel like you are snatching away their prized and powerful *Liliana of the Veil* planeswalker card for no reason. Communication is always best practice in any parenting endeavor.

Apart from the potentially racy themes, parents are most concerned with the financial burden MTG. Part of the fun of TCGs is the card collection itself, but every new set of cards costs money and it is impossible to collect each card in the set by purchasing one, two, or a dozen packs of cards from your neighborhood's Local Friendly Game Store (LFGS).

Card packs (booster packs, boosters) in TCGs operate like lotteries. They have a few random cards from a specific set inside with small chances to contain rare or powerful cards. In *Magic*, booster packs contain fifteen playable cards, while each set contains around 200-300 unique cards on average. Even if a collector struck the one-in-a-billion odds of pulling fifteen unique cards every single time they bought a booster, they would still have to spend $4 per pack around twenty times to complete a set. Realistically, collectors would have to spend hundreds or even thousands of dollars to complete a set by opening booster packs.

Players can buy MTG starter kits for around ten dollars, but these collections hold the bare minimum amount of cards required to build a deck. One starter kit leaves little room for players to customize their decks, drastically reducing their ability to strategize or adjust play style. A few booster packs might diversify the deck, but at $4 a pop minimum and no guarantee of pulling "good" cards, deck building can get expensive. *Fast*.

There are online versions of most TCGs available for free or "freemium," meaning free to download with optional (strongly encouraged) in-game purchases. *Magic: The Gathering Arena* and *Pokémon TCG Online* are two examples of online TCGs. These online versions can serve as a great way to learn the game without investing money in the games' card collection aspect. If you want to get familiar with MTG rules to play alongside your child, take a look at the online battle options. Who knows? Maybe your child will prefer the online version of MTG because they gain the ability to play wherever, whenever, without the responsibility of a tangible deck. Still, some collectors prefer the look, feel, and potential value of tangible decks, like some avid readers prefer paperbacks to Kindles.

Some collectors prefer real-life cards for the resale value. The secondary market for rare trading cards can be lucrative and some collectors use the booster packs' lottery system to try and win big. *Pokémon: TCG's* VMAX Rainbow Holo Charizard from the Burning Shadows set sells for about $300 on eBay, while a PSA 10 (mint condition) first edition base set Charizard sells for around $300,000 as of 2021.[16] The elusive Black Lotus card in *Magic* is the rarest card in the game and a copy signed by the original artist sold in 2021 for $511,100.[17] People searching for rare, valuable cards justify the exorbitant amount of money they spend on booster packs the same way people who buy lottery tickets do: there is a small chance they will strike gold and be set for life.

Not every parent wants to introduce their kids to the lottery. Parents should teach their children how to limit their spending on TCGs by creating boundaries around purchases. We can educate our children about money by demonstrating how to set budgets for small, obtainable goals, like affording a handful of MTG booster pack purchases by the end of the month.

---

[16] https://www.pricecharting.com/game/pokemon-base-set/charizard-1st-edition-4#completed-auctions-manual-only

[17] https://www.polygon.com/2021/1/27/22253079/magic-the-gathering-black-lotus-auction-price-2021

If financial comprehension is not in the cards for your family, you can also implement a reward system. If your child had great behavior all week, treat them to a booster pack! It costs about as much as a movie rental or a few scoops of ice cream, and the cards will last a lot longer. If your child brushes their teeth, puts on their PJs, and gets in bed without you asking, reward them with a quick battle in place of their bedtime story. Positive reinforcement can help your child feel recognized for their good behavior.

MAGIC: THE BENEFITTING

Now, with several concrete methods to mitigate potential drawbacks of TCGs, we can dive into the multitude of benefits they can provide our children. The more the player participates in the game and its community, the greater the benefits. Even entry-level players who collect *Magic* cards for the artwork benefit. It might not seem like collectors experience developmental rewards, but there are plenty. All players, collectors and competitors alike, can take pride in their decks.

Magic has thousands of cards from different sets released since the game's inception. Endless combinations allow for virtually every player to construct their own unique deck. Many *Magic* players take pride in their decks because they spent time and resources building them and maintaining them. Dr. Theodore explains that many MTG players' personal decks become representations of themselves. Even for players who simply collect the prettiest or coolest cards, their deck functions as artistic expression.

Competitive players can take deeper pride in their decks. When most people first start playing MTG (including me), they fall into the trap of creating an overpowered, offensive deck. However, if they rely only on powerful attack cards, they are missing important components for battle. The power is great as long as you also have the energy cards or support cards to play them. They are not powerful enough on their own. New players must learn to balance their main deck to be powerful *and* responsive.

Some dedicated players are proud of decks that showcase skills they find impressive or powerful, which gives us as parents insight into their perception of strength and strategy. Players take pride in their stronger combinations when they defeat an opponent. They want to build internal pride, so they strive to adjust their strategies to gain more success. With great power comes great responsibility, and the responsibility of building and maintaining a TCG deck makes kids feel powerful.

Another benefit of *Magic* is how it promotes social development. Some kids have not developed their social skills enough to make new friends effortlessly. MTG and other TCGs give shyer kids a shared interest to bond over. The *Magic* community is famously welcoming, and kids who meet people through MTG get buddies to meet up with for conventions, competitions, and expansion deck prereleases. Plus, other players can give your child pointers on becoming stronger. Listening to mentors and mentoring others in the community engages amazing social skills like how to be patient and understanding when transferring knowledge.

Magic players' internal sense of power is bolstered when they participate in the game's community. Beginners might feel a little bit stuck on level one, but as they practice and improve their deck, they will gain experience and win more battles. Learning how to improve a little every day is a skill our children can apply to nearly every facet of their lives.

Players can independently explore MTG's play styles to improve their success, too. A player might begin with the Red style, which is an aggressive, offense style built for quick destruction. However, after repeatedly losing to heavily defensive players, they might switch to the Blue style to mimic the strategy continuously beating them.

The turn-based style of TCGs allows for critical thinking through engagement with offense and defense tactics. Every attack in *Magic* can be defended with a sacrifice, so players must weigh the pros and cons of defending or attacking on the playing field. Engaging in strategy-based games helps children weigh odds and develop their judgment skills.

Game study and practice help the player build their strategy from one-attack turns to multi-spell, multi-attack rounds designed to devastate opponents. The power behind the attack feels good, and the opponent, as a member of the community, will recognize the turn as cunning. As your child wins more competitions, they will feel a sense of well-earned pride and accomplishment invaluable to their development.

MAGIC: THE THERAPIZING

We can also use the competitive environment TCGs take place in to mimic real-world conflict. I use a basic fifty-two-card deck to introduce my clients to card games' potential therapeutic uses.

When I played with a client I will call Jake, I took a fifty-two-card French deck and dealt myself all the high cards (Jacks through Aces) right in front of him, then dealt the rest to him. I told him we are both going to flip a card and the highest card wins. After losing a few rounds, he was understandably confused and a little upset.

"Why are we playing this?" he groaned. "What's the point of this game if I obviously can't win?"

Jake experienced some friction with his parents where he felt helpless, like he could not win. He had not yet connected the dots, so I laid the point out for him.

"That's a great metaphor for what's going on at home right now, right? If you can't win, why try? Let's see how you can still win…"

We moved into a contextual game, where I told Jake he could play a total of three cards to form a party and defeat my powerful card. I flipped a Queen and Jake responded with a six, three, and four. "All together that's thirteen!" he grinned. "It beats your Queen!"

We went on like this for a few rounds, where Jake had up to three cards overcome my high card. If he pulled a pair of nines, I lost right away. If he pulled a two, a three, and a four to total nine, I would win with my high cards. The purpose was not to teach Jake he could win every time with three cards, it was to teach him he *could* win. And statistically, three random cards beat a high card most of the time. After he felt more empowered, we discussed how the card game relates to his life.

Each card represents a person Jake can turn to for help. They are people he can trust to build his strength and overcome stronger obstacles he cannot defeat on his own. Jake listed possible party members from his own life: family, friends, teachers, and me. The card game helped Jake visualize who he can rely on and utilize when he feels overwhelmed.

I use this strategy with many clients. Once they are comfortable with the fifty-two-card format, I overlay the concepts from the fifty-two-card game on more complicated games with extra barriers, like energy and environmental impact cards from *Magic*. My monster might be more powerful than theirs, but they can place more Land cards to generate more resources to spend on more spells to take me down. Sometimes they win and sometimes they lose, but we practice persistence and keep playing with new strategies until they feel confident in their problem-solving skills.

If a child feels weak in the real world, we can explore those feelings from a safe distance with card games. Jake did not feel like he had any support in his party, but once we stopped discussing people and started discussing cards, he was able to see how different people in his life functioned the same way. When we move to MTG and use energy to summon support, we discuss how summoning help can take up emotional energy, especially if we are too proud to expend it.

Magic's different play styles can function as therapeutic devices as well. Each play style has benefits and drawbacks we can compare to conflict-resolution styles. The aggressive Red style might be good for obliterating opponents, but it does not exemplify how to engage with others. The defensive Blue style might seem tempting, but when we consider its weaknesses, we realize defensive strategies around communication can leave both people unheard in a dialogue. The White and Green style—the two most balanced—can counterbalance each other to help MTG fans improve their communication skills.

The benefits of cards for children are as limitless as the different games we can play with them. It is one of the main reasons we decided to release common therapeutic techniques in geek culture as a deck of cards. They are versatile, easily accessible, and familiar for most people. To date, they have been highly acclaimed and well-received by parents, educators, geeks, and clinicians alike. Cards, card games, and TCGs can help us relate to our children in therapeutic "gamemodes."

MAGIC: THE ENGAGING

We can engage our children with *Magic* and other TCGs by picking up a deck and getting in touch with our own inner child. A round of *Magic*, *Pokémon: TCG*, or *Yu-Gi-Oh* only takes about twenty minutes to half an hour depending on the play style, so the games are easy to sneak into daily routines, one round at a time. You can use online versions of games to play with your kids, but if you would rather play at the table, some TCG kits come ready for multiplayer battles, like *Pokémon Battle Academy*. You might even discover some cards are too cute *not* to collect while you are playing.

The basic rules for most card games (the objective, turn options, and restrictions) are simple enough to understand beforehand. The barrier of entry for card games is one of the lowest for geek culture activities. Most parents have been playing *Uno, War, Rummy*, and other card games for years, so they understand card games' basic flow.

Once you understand the flow and general game rules, more complex rules unique to each type or card are usually referenced right under the artwork. Anyone who has played a card game before has probably nodded off during the initial rule-reading—we know the best way to learn is to play!

Your local friendly game shop most likely loves teaching the basics of the game to players who need some extra help. Most are so excited to welcome new members to the *Magic* community that they give away free starter decks! You can check their schedule of events for MTG Game Nights and bring your child to play together. MTG players can play on the same team when four or more players compete, which is one of the amazing benefits the game offers its players. Battling on the same team as your child might help you learn while it helps them feel important.

We want to keep in mind the barriers our kids face when they learn to play *Magic* and apply them to ourselves as well. We are not going to be Master Planeswalkers in our first battle. We are going to struggle to pronounce Borborygmos and Fblthp (yes, that is a real MTG card) when we play them. We might feel confused or frustrated. We might even feel the urge to give up, but if we did, we would be setting a bad example.

Instead of quitting and discouraging our child's interest, we can open a discourse. We can tell our children even the parents get frustrated sometimes too, especially when learning new concepts. We can even ask their advice on how to feel better as a newcomer to TCG.

To engage with TCGs, we have to access our inner child. Children want to discover the world around them. They want to learn everything and know everything because it is all still exciting. When we tap into our inner child, we can explore new concepts while encouraging the same exploration in our kids. We can even encourage them to take on the role of mentor and lead us and our new deck to victory.

CHAPTER 6

COSPLAY, LARPING, & FAN FICTION

"Most of the people you see going to work today are LARPing an incredibly boring RPG called 'professionalism.'"
— Cory Doctorow, In Real Life

We have covered the basic genres of geek culture, and now we can explore them a bit deeper. For example, in *Dungeons & Dragons* (D&D) players act as their characters through role-play. The success of the campaign relies on immersion, improvisation, and engagement. Role-playing has its benefits, but what we might not expect is for our child to become so attached to their D&D character they start writing stories about their adventures outside of group sessions. They renamed one of their toys from "Teddy" to "Xarlax the Zealous" after their in-game character and play with it constantly. They even asked for chainmail and a set of horns for their Halloween costume. Are they falling too far down the geek culture rabbit hole?

The short answer is no. They are simply so engaged in their character, they are diving deeper into geek culture to the levels of **cosplay**, **LARPing**, and **fan fiction**.

Fan fiction, LARPing, and cosplay can sound like foreign concepts to most parents because they are not as mainstream as video games, or even anime. They may seem like "advanced" geek culture, or geek culture on steroids, but when we break them down we can see they are simply niche versions of regular activities people do every day.

COSPLAY

Costume play, or "cosplay" for short, is a self-explanatory term. The official definition is "the activity or practice of dressing up as a character from a work of fiction such as a comic book, video game, or television show."[18] Most of our children (and probably their parents) participate in cosplay for Halloween. My son has cosplayed as Spider-Man, Charizard, and other fictional characters to go trick-or-treating. If your kids look forward to dressing up on Halloween or wearing their fairy wings to the grocery store, they are already fans of cosplaying.

As we grow up, cosplaying tends to stop being encouraged as a form of play. Adult dress-up becomes bound to Halloween and Comic Conventions (comic-cons). It is not socially acceptable to leave the house dressed as a superhero or a woodland fairy, no matter how magical or powerful it makes you feel. We must find empowerment through more palatable wardrobe options.

Studies have shown wearing clothes that make you feel important or intelligent can improve cognitive functioning and change how you interact with others. The way we feel about ourselves is directly linked to our appearance, whether we notice it or not.[19] A new power skirt or fresh-pressed suit for work might make us feel more capable of taking on a presentation, and a new princess dress or hero's cape can have the same empowering effect for our little ones.

Cosplay allows people of all ages to identify with a favorite character. Kids can look at them and say, "I like this person, I want to be like them." They can then mimic the character's appearance

---

[18] "Cosplay Definition & Meaning." Merriam-Webster. Merriam-Webster. Accessed December 14, 2021. https://www.merriam-webster.com/dictionary/cosplay.

[19] Barker, Erin T, and Marc H Bornstein. "Global Self-Esteem, Appearance Satisfaction, and Self-Reported Dieting in Early Adolescence." The Journal of early adolescence. U.S. National Library of Medicine, April 1, 2010. https://www.ncbi.nlm.nih.gov/pmc/articles/PMC3496262/.

to feel closer to them. Their cosplay might be a suit of armor, a steampunk outfit, or simply a dressier, business look that makes them feel like Clark Kent hiding Superman's identity.

Adults and children alike engage in cosplay any time they pick out a costume for a party or a special event. Some kids cosplay as brides and grooms from their favorite love stories, while others might combine their two (or three, or four) favorite fictional characters' looks to create their very own character. Cosplay allows us to step into the shoes of our heroes to look and feel as cool as they do on the big screen. So, why are we limiting the fun to one day a year? To understand how we can extend the benefits of cosplay, we must explore its close relative, LARPing.

LIVE-ACTION ROLE-PLAYING (LARPING)

When my son dresses up as Spider-Man for Halloween, he is cosplaying. When he puts on his Spider-Man costume at home and shoots me with silly string, howling, "I got you! You're stuck in my web!" he is LARPing, or "live-action role-playing." He does not believe he is wearing Spider-Man's outfit at that moment—he believes he *is* Spider-Man.

The term LARPing originally only referred to war-reenactors in parks and Shakespearian festivals. In more recent history, the term has grown and can now reference many more activities. As of 2021, the official definition for LARPing from Oxford Languages is: "a form of interactive role-playing game in which the participants portray characters through physical action, often in costume and with props."[20] LARPing is a term used lovingly by geeks, but derogatorily by people outside of geek culture. However, people

---

[20] "Oxford Languages and Google - English." Oxford Languages: LARP definition. Oxford University Press. Accessed December 14, 2021. https://languages.oup.com/google-dictionary-en/.

Fan fiction does not exist solely in writing, although it is most commonly found as written word. Our kids create fanfic when they play with dolls from fictional worlds. We even make our own fan fiction as adults without even noticing. When we question what Spider-Man would do if he had to face Batman, or what the Founding Fathers would think of our last few presidents, we are making up scenarios for pre-existing characters. We are creating our own fan fiction.

As geek culture activities, cosplay, LARPing, and fan fiction each have their roots in common childhood experiences. Most of us have lost our inclination to play with themes, characters, and stories from our early exploration days, but geek culture embraces play from childhood all the way into adulthood. Unfortunately, the perception of these forms of play as childlike has hindered most parents from embracing the many benefits.

Cosplay, LARPing, and fan fiction have faced their own moral panics similar to the ones surrounding other forms of geek culture. When children engage with imaginative activities, parents grow concerned their little ones will be exposed to concepts like erotica, violence, or forms of intolerance before the parents have a chance to explain them in detail at a chosen time.

Even when playtime is monitored, parents still worry their child is directing energy into frivolous, time-wasting hobbies. Children pour hours of their time into making up stories with toys instead of finishing their homework. We might cringe every time we buy them material to build a new costume. We might even get frustrated by our own parental fanfic fantasy of the child prodigies we could raise if our kids spent as much time on their studies as they spent in their head. Little do we know, these hobbies provide as much productivity for childhood development as school work... they might even be *more* important than homework.

EARNING EXPERIENCE: DEVELOPMENT THROUGH PLAY

Childhood play teaches a wide variety of skills from welding to empathetic reasoning. Imaginative play increases cognitive ability, social skills, self-worth, self-identity, mood regulation, and more. When kids operate in a free, uninhibited environment, they gravitate toward their most authentic self. There are no two better ways to get to know your child than to watch them play, and play *with* them. Even when they cosplay as a dragon or LARPing as an astronaut, they make decisions based on what feels natural to them. You will experience firsthand who they are at their core without outside stress affecting their in-game choices.

PRACTICAL SKILLS

The LARPers and cosplayers I know are the most creative, handy, and skilled people I have ever met. Building homemade costumes for Comic-Cons and other LARPing events is an intricate, hands-on process. It is not uncommon for a seasoned cosplayer to practice sewing, welding, and woodworking. They know basic coding for the flashing LED lights woven into their costumes. They can carve, stain, and seal weapons. Some are better with a steel forge than a soccer ball. By building costumes for events in their community, they can also pick up valuable social and entrepreneurial skills to apply to other areas in their lives.

Exploring the many practical skills cosplay has to offer can help a child explore potential career paths in fun and engaging ways. Your child might discover they hate working with fabric, but love welding and metalworking. This might spark an interest in mechanical engineering. If they enjoy programming LEDs and

protects him. Your child might want to slay a dragon, but we know Harry would rather protect the magical beasts. Thus, your child can learn to put aside their own wants to keep playing the role honestly, which improves their empathy and critical decision-making processes.

Fan fiction is another great way for young geeks to feel powerful. Crafting stories can be difficult, especially for young storytellers. Fanfic writers are free to be creative without the initial hurdles of character building or setting development. Young storytellers can take well-known, comforting characters and guide them on completely new and exciting adventures. Without knowing it, your child might be creating fan fictions to help them accept, reject, or challenge certain aspects of their life through familiar characters.

Fanfic creators can use their works as a form of self-reflection. They can examine what the heroes' journey looks like in their story and ask self-critical questions. Maybe it is important that the villain is a math teacher and the bridge troll has the same name as their sister. Self-reflection is a part of growth and should be encouraged in children who build stories through fan fiction. This reflection can have notable payoffs when your kids start spending more time in their social circles.

SOCIAL SKILLS

LARPers and cosplayers participate in their communities as much as they craft. They all share an interest in the creation process and role-playing fun, even if they do not have a shared favorite movie, TV series, or comic book. Some fans attend comic-cons with repair kits and set up booths to conduct free repairs for their peers' costumes. This gives them an opportunity to bolster others in their community while also bending their ears for tips, tricks, and strategies.

Cosplay and LARPing are extremely collaborative communities. YouTube, Tumblr, and Reddit are full of people who share how-to videos for constructing cosplay outfits. LARP and cosplay participants also share their own ideas and learn to improve from other members, and that openness is encouraged.

Some shyer children may not find sharing with a stranger how they built their costume so simple, but there are other ways to engage in cosplay communities. Cosplay makes it easier for people to identify their "tribe" through costumes. A *Star Trek* fan (also known as a Trekkie) can easily spot other Trekkies by their outfits and strike up conversations about the latest release from the *Star Trek* universe. Any social barrier of entry to community is broken down through a common interest, making social interactions easier for new or shy cosplayers.

Studies have shown that individuals who played make-believe as children show better competence, cognitive capabilities, and empathetic attunement than those who did not.[21] Participating in fantasy role-playing, cosplay, creative storytelling, and other forms of play help our children grow into strong, healthy, capable adults. We can also use them to teach our children valuable lessons they can carry into adulthood, like the importance of consent.

TEACHING CONSENT

One of the ways LARPing and cosplay can be beneficial, especially to adolescents, is through meaningful interactions in a safe space. Preteens and teenagers can experience flirting and romance without risking their safety and emotional wellbeing. In tabletop role-playing games (TTRPGs) like D&D and supervised LARP ses-

---

[21] Lillard A.S., Pinkham A.M., & Smith E. (2011). Pretend play and cognitive development. In: Goswami U, ed. Handbook of Childhood Cognitive Development. 2nd ed. London: Blackwell; 285–311.

trouble accepting them, he can remove himself from the game or seek advice from supervisors. This works similarly if genders are reversed.

Legitimate LARPs and conventions have safety mechanics in place to protect the players. Most LARPs, especially LARPs taking place over multiple days, begin with a safety and consent seminar. In these introductory sessions, facilitators discuss the safety mechanics and calibration tools players can implement to ensure their comfort. The safety features give players the ability to step back if a LARPing session becomes too intense, uncomfortable, or emotionally difficult.

Examples of the safety features and mechanics present as most LARPs include a "door is always open" policy, meaning a player can leave the experience at any time for any reason, no questions asked. Most LARPs employ safe words or symbols to signal a player's discomfort with new in-game content. If players are sitting around a table, an index card with a large "X" is placed in the center within reach of everyone. If a player decides to make a romantic advance on another player and anyone touches the "X card," the advance is denied and disappears from play without argument. In a more physically involved LARP with players running around in a space, "X arms" can replace the "X card." If a player runs into the room announcing his wife was attacked by pirates and another player makes an "X" with their arms, the introduced information is immediately wiped from the story, no explanation necessary.

Fan fiction sites have types of consent available to readers and writers as well. Because so many fanfic writers use the medium for catharsis and self-reflection, fan fiction can contain some inappropriate content. Sites that host fanfics actively create and improve methods to prevent audiences from reading uncomfortable topics. Archive of Our Own, Wattpad, and FanFiction.net have maturity ratings on their stories and include tags for their topics. The reader can only access mature stories by giving their consent to access the information.

There is a cultural shift in place as our society places more weight on the presence of consent than ever before. We can use methods found in LARPing, cosplay, and fan fiction to teach consent to our children. When we explore each of these activities in a therapeutic setting, we see how their teachings can improve our children's development even further.

BENEFITS IN A THERAPEUTIC SETTING

LARPing, cosplay, and fan fiction can be used in a therapeutic setting when the events taking place in the pretend worlds correlate to what the client needs to work on in real life, like finding themselves, dealing with trauma, and exploring real-world consequences.

A common therapy trope in TV shows and movies is role-playing, where a couple, a parent and child, or two friends will pretend to be the other to point out flaws in their reasoning. These scenes usually escalate to full-on mockery and fighting. While we absolutely use role-playing or LARPing in a therapeutic way, it does not play out as dramatically.

Gestalt theory explores the human mind as parts of a whole, gives clinicians like me the Empty Chair Technique. This is a practice where I place an empty chair across the room from my client and ask them to have a conversation with an imaginary person sitting in it. The imaginary person is a part of them. It might be their biggest fear, their critical inner voice, or their dislike of peanut butter. They LARP a scenario to communicate with a part of their identity they want to see change or improve, which encourages more progress than simply saying, "I want to like peanut butter, but I can't."

worrying about a wrong move capable of throwing our life out of balance. We deserve catharsis, and playing through fantasy worlds can help us experience it in a safe, low-consequence world.

If you would like an introduction to the world of LARPing and fan fiction before diving into conventions and writing events, look no further than your own master of fantasy, your child. If they like to play with dolls or toy tools, offer to join in their game. If they want to play outside, pick up a stick and ask them what it could be. Is it a sword? A fishing rod? A magic wand? The game is starting already!

We can encourage their play by asking guiding questions without steering their imagination in any specific direction. The magic words we clinicians use are, "I wonder what you'll do next!" This encourages the creator to consider all possible steps forward without using any words to accidentally (or purposely) force their story to progress in ways we think are best.

Cosplay is an easy activity to explore because we already do it once a year on Halloween. Instead of purchasing pre-assembled costumes, head to your local craft store and see how you and your child can work together to build a unique costume for Halloween. Cosplay supplies are becoming more widely available. Even big box stores like Michaels and JoAnn Fabrics have sections for cosplay materials like thermoplastics and wire lights. Maybe you could even build a matching costume and explore cosplay together!

The most important way to engage your child is to encourage their naturally imaginative mind and help them explore potential outlets for their creativity. We want to allow our children to learn their own interests and hobbies through exposure and engagement. Fictional worlds created by others help our children stay engaged with interesting elements of the mythology. They are interested in magic and power, but they are learning about friendship, persistence, responsibility, and self-actualization.

So, where does all this magic and power come from? How do all these stories interact with one another? Why do some characters have super powers and others do not? We are going to explore these questions in our next chapter. Whether your kid loves the Smurfs or the Ewoks, we are going to get to the bottom of where all these fictional characters are born and how they make their way into our hearts.

While Gloria from *Colossal* was a grownup with a literal monster to overcome, adult stressors can be more figuratively intimidating. How have we learned to overcome loftier fears of debt, taxes, and negative self-talk? What did we use to overcome them? Our childhood fantasy play and heroism undoubtedly plays a part for other real life monsters or life problems.

Maybe we played Cops and Robbers with our neighbors as kids, staying up late at night waving flashlights around the shadows. Maybe we were invested in erecting blanket forts in our living rooms. Maybe we built spaceships out of cardboard and aluminum to confront aliens from outer space. We played as heroes and triumphed over imaginary versions of our own fears—because why would we ever lose at our own made up games? We learned about different monsters from bedtime stories and TV shows, and used them to create imaginary villains of our own to fight against. We did not realize it at the time, but we were training ourselves for the battles to come in adulthood.

We must let children do the same, so when they enter adulthood and experience *really* scary situations, our kids know how to face them. Children are far more likely to respond to obstacles with a "fight" response when obstacles resemble the dragons and aliens from their play. Children play and simulate real-life stress the same way we dip our toes in the water before diving into a pool. It is a way to familiarize ourselves with danger before we face it head on.

Heroic fantasy play gives players extra power and abilities to face ferocious fears. Magic spells, suits of armor, or super-strength lets children fight off foes with a little more power than we would experience in the real world. Children's opponents can be horror movie monsters, video game bosses, or creatures built from their imagination. When the child succeeds in taking down their fake foe, they create success-based confidence and a verifiable sense of accomplishment. Such positive experiences from play have real-world applications when children have the chance to play safely and win.

Studies conducted on play and make-believe demonstrate people who have better fantasy and imaginative abilities show better social competence, cognitive capabilities, and empathetic attunement to others.[23] Fantasy play allows children to imagine social roles for make-believe friends, solve puzzles in fictional dungeons, and work together with other kids to feel important and accomplished. In fact, repressing play and imaginative expression can have detrimental effects on the cognitions, behaviors, and emotional outcomes of children.

Oftentimes our childhood games involve struggles with imaginary bad guys. We fight them with vigor and emerge victorious, but man, *what a fight!* Dramatic, fictional battles and conflicts with villains give children a safe space to confront their monsters, learn their weaknesses, and develop strategies to win the battle.

Remember playing freeze tag with your friends? The game was simple enough: tag another person to freeze them in place. If all the players are frozen in three minutes, you win! As more kids played the game and spread it around the world, new players added rules. Players could unfreeze other players. Home bases were added, and touching a base made players immune to freezing. Now the players who are "it" have more to overcome to win. They have to find creative ways to get around the new obstacles.

No children get hurt during the average game of freeze tag. The "ice" existed in the players' imaginations. Through make-believe play like this, the players learn methods to appraise their situation and use tools at their disposal to overcome obstacles and win.

Humans have been building simple games and stories out of imagined monsters, magical creatures, and other fictional concepts since the beginning of recorded history. We warn children of outside dangers in engaging ways by manifesting monsters to

---

[23] Lillard A.S., Pinkham A.M., & Smith E. (2011). Pretend play and cognitive development. In: Goswami U, ed. Handbook of Childhood Cognitive Development. 2nd ed. London: Blackwell; 285–311.

pian, futuristic setting focused on a "combination of lowlife and high tech" featuring advanced technological and scientific achievements, such as Artificial Intelligence (AI) and cybernetics. The genre tends to be less apologetic in its portrayal of adult themes, but at the same time takes real-world questions of technology, government, and death to deep and insightful levels. For example, *Blade Runner* explores what it means to be a human when AI androids fight for human rights in a dystopian future setting.

Sometimes it can be difficult to tell the differences between fantasy and science fiction stories. They can usually be spotted through the origin of their fictional elements. Science fiction uses exaggerations of science and technology present in our world, while fantasy operates with a scientifically impossible set of rules and history. For example, the movie *Eternal Sunshine of the Spotless Mind* uses a scientific, medical procedure to erase memories, while *Harry Potter* has magic to erase memories when witches or wizards say the spell, "Obliviate." Both processes accomplish the same results, but one is considered science fiction and the other fantasy.

We want to know the difference between the two so we can better engage with our children. Not all geeks are into science fiction *and* fantasy, just like not all sports fans watch hockey and football. The nuances separating the genres come down to a matter of interest. Some kids would be more excited to receive a copy of *The Hobbit* than *Cloud Atlas* for their birthday, and that is okay. The more familiar we are with the differences between the two genres, the more we can choose the right material for engagement.

Even if it's difficult to tell fantasy and science fiction apart, most fictional stories in geek culture fit into either one or both genres. Some stories are easy to sort right away, like the examples given above. Classic fairy tales like *Cinderella* and *Rumplestiltskin* are also fantasy stories. Other stories are a little more difficult to classify, like the stories running through the Marvel Cinematic Universe (MCU).

The MCU started out as cut-and-dry science fiction. Cyborg Iron Man, the science-gone-wrong Hulk, and even Norse princes Thor and Loki explain away their super-powers as "ancient science" from their planet. It was not until *Doctor Strange's* release in 2016 that the universe took a nosedive from science fiction to fantasy. MCU's creative team cleverly explored the universe's magic through a science-minded character. The character of Dr. Strange struggled with magic's existence alongside the MCU's fanbase. Since the magical floodgates opened, we have seen witches, wizards, and ancient spells in the MCU.

Other, modern fiction stories flirt with the boundary between science fiction and fantasy. The differences between the genres are not as important as the implications their elements have on our children. While science fiction focuses on what *could* exist in our world, and fantasy explores impossible magic and magical creatures, both are centered around values like friendship, family, humanity, and what it means to be alive.

FALLING DOWN THE RABBIT HOLE

Almost every fictional medium uses science fiction and fantasy: books, movies, TV series, video games, D&D, plays, musicals, and more. How is a parent supposed to protect their children from overindulging in make-believe concepts with such pervasive roots?

The Netflix fantasy series *Hilda* explores this question. Hilda's mother tries to protect her from the fantasy creatures around their home in the Wilderness. She moves Hilda to Trolberg, a city with a thick wall built to protect citizens from dangerous Wilderness creatures. The rest of the show follows young Hilda as she finds ways to skirt the wall and form relationships with fantasy beings. Her mother tries to stop her so she can lead a "normal"

Psychologist Deena Weisberg notes, "Children in the banana-as-telephone game do not end up with mistaken beliefs either about bananas' communicative abilities or the edibility of telephones."[28] Children learn symbolic understanding through play, and despite the fears some parents have, they come out the other side with a firm grasp of playtime versus real-world problem solving.

As parents, we want to be available to our children for discussions surrounding reality and fantasy. Your child might not immediately understand that although their stick acts as a sword during playtime, it cannot be used to intimidate the family dog. Maybe our kids need some debriefing after more in-depth play sessions to keep them from climbing their dresser like a beanstalk. If it seems like your child seems confused about the lines between reality and fantasy, it is a good opportunity to engage them in conversation. We can set boundaries around appropriate times and places for fantasy play. When we enact boundaries, we set our children up for success by encouraging their imagination and laying out realistic expectations for them to meet.

The best way to build healthy boundaries around fantasy and heroic play for your child is to jump in the game and play with them! Pirates always need good, strong crew members and Hydras have a tendency to keep their heads up in battle. By participating in the play, you can monitor their exploration and gently guide them back into reality when playtime is over.

When playtime is over, we can discuss the concepts our children explored and discover how imaginative adventures translate into real-life situations. If our child has a habit of pretending they are invisible, use it to discuss *why* they feel like they do not want to be seen sometimes. Maybe they feel like they are lacking some independence and would love to have some alone time. Then we can discuss what being invisible means for people who love them

---

[28] Weisberg, D. S. (2015). Pretend play. *Wiley Interdisciplinary Reviews. Cognitive Science, 6*, 3.

and cannot find them, and the stress their invisibility might unintentionally put on their friends and family.

Instead of discouraging fantasy play, we as parents can use some of fantasy's most engaging concepts to teach our children about the world. Collaborative, imaginative play is beneficial for children and keeps them engaged, stimulated, and curious about the world around them.

FROM PADAWAN TO JEDI MASTER THROUGH HEROIC PLAY

Our job as parents is to guide our children toward difficult moral questions and help them find answers.

Humanity reaches morality through storytelling, and some of life's most confounding questions are explored through fantasy and science fiction. For proof, look no further than fairy tales. We might not have fire-breathing dragons or intelligent droid interpreters in the real world, but the stories with these fictional characters are still exploring real world struggles. Even stories full of witches, trolls, giants, and mermaids traverse through a human experience that resonates with the audience. One of the greatest contemporary producers of fairy tales is Disney.

Most Disney and Pixar movies take place in fantasy or science fiction settings full of talking animals and magic. Their stories are popular with young minds because they explore relatable experiences through engaging premises. Disney's *The Little Mermaid* is an adaptation of an original Hans Christian Andersen fairy tale of the same name. (The original is pretty gruesome, so Disney lightened it up a little.) Even though most of the story takes place underwater through mermaid royalty, it still teaches valuable lessons about love, friendship, family, and trust.

with kindness and empathy for people different from them. We all know the world needs more kindness and empathy, and encouraging these traits in our children creates the lasting change we as parents are trying to instill in the next generation.

HEROES NEVER LEAVE A PROBLEM UNSOLVED

Kids have big feelings, and whether our little ones are happy, sad, angry, or scared, we are going to hear about it. From infancy, most times our kids act out are times when they feel like they are missing something. They might be missing food, sleep, or context for a problem, but they are not equipped to express their need rationally yet. They might not even know what they need at that moment. All they know is they are missing *something* and the feeling is upsetting. Fantasy play can help them develop skills to identify and communicate their needs more effectively.

On a recent Taco Tuesday at home, my son slumped into his chair at the dinner table. His unusually long day left him tired and irritable. I tried to engage him in conversation, but he was a ball of mumbles and sighs. I left him alone to eat his taco. He picked it up, pulled it toward his mouth…and cracked the shell, spilling its contents back onto his plate in a sad heap.

He started *wailing*.

Some parents might see their children have this type of reaction and view it as "overly emotional" or "a fit over something small," but this view does not help the situation. It only belittles the feelings our children have in these important parenting moments.

His frustration was not only about the taco. I knew that. He had hit his emotional limit for the day and the taco sent him over the edge. My first instinct was to dash into the kitchen for a new shell to conduct emergency taco surgery, but I resisted. Instead, I looked down at my own plate. I waited until he looked away and smashed my own taco shell to bits.

"Oh no!" I wailed, "*Now* what do I do? My taco is ruined!"

My son looked up at me and saw the despair on my face. He quickly stopped crying and reached his hand out toward me.

"No, Daddy," he said with a sniffle, "it's okay. You can still eat it."

"What do you mean?" I hollered, "*It's destroyed! I'll never eat another taco again!*" mimicking what he has just done a moment ago.

He giggled now, catching on a little bit.

"It's not destroyed, Daddy. You can still eat it."

"How?"

My son squished his sad taco pile into the center of his plate and scooped it into his mouth. I copied him, and we finished our tacos together because of his genius problem-solving skills.

We can apply my taco-self-destruction technique to encourage problem-solving thinking in other situations as well. Instead of a Mexican food explosion, we can use fantasy and science fiction stories to show our kids how to solve problems or recover from them. When your child slips while playing outside and rips a hole in their shirt, we can use their favorite character to help them forward.

"I wonder what *insert favorite hero here* would do if their costume got ripped during battle. Would a hero stop fighting and run away? Or would they brush off the dust and jump right back in?"

Fantasy and science fiction heroes are masters at creative problem-solving, and they are more humanized than ever before in our current mythologies. The more our kids engage with them, the more they learn to think on their feet and find out-of-the-box solutions to problems. The characters from these genres empower our children and make them feel even more accomplished by acting the way their heroes act. We can encourage a productive thought process and help our children develop confident, clever solutions to whatever life throws at them.

HEROES COME TO THE RESCUE

I used heroic play with a client, named Peter, to help him understand the role others play in his life. He was only eight years old when he first came to me. His parents were in the middle of a nasty divorce and nastier custody battle. Peter felt lost, and he was struggling to understand the world around him. I talked to him about what he did in his spare time and he told me he liked video games, especially a game called *Garry's Mod*.

Well, *Garry's Mod* is tricky to use in therapy because it is a sandbox game. These games have no set objectives, stories, or characters. Sandbox games exist specifically for free play and heavy customizations. Still, I was determined to engage with Peter on his level, so we played *Garry's Mod* together for our first few sessions.

We built different characters together and talked about their traits. Peter built a sharpshooter type, a fighter type, a ranger type, and a few more characters, and his mood at the start of our sessions determined which he would play as. We talked about how their unique traits feel more or less helpful depending on how Peter felt each day.

One day, Peter came in and surprised me.

"I built a hero," he said.

"Tell me all about it!" I replied immediately.

We explored this new "hero" character together. I asked him about what makes him strong, what makes him weak, and what he does as a hero. He told me his hero always appeared in times of need, ready to fight for anyone that needed him. We talked about what the dark side of this hero might look like and whether he had any villainous tendencies. Peter did not believe his hero could do anything *too* bad—he is a hero, after all.

We talked about Peter's hero until we realized he had modeled it after his dad. This hero symbolized much of what his dad had done for him since the custody battle began. He trusted his dad to come fight for him when his life got too hard to manage on his own. It is not uncommon for kids to use heroic play to model people in their real life as well as fictional heroes, and Peter had done this with his father.

I was summoned to testify on Peter's behalf during the custody hearings. I was able to show the judge the characteristics Peter used to define his father as the same ones we clinicians use to determine whether a child feels safe at home. Our work with heroic play revealed Peter's recognition of "good" and "bad" traits and could tell them apart, and he believed his dad to be the "good" (better) influence on his life. Peter's dad won custody and Peter got to continue playing at home in a safe environment.

Kids must feel safe in their environment to engage in heroic and fantasy play. If children do not feel safe enough to engage, they miss out on the development opportunities that kind of play awards them. It is important for us as parents to ensure our children's safety and comfort while they explore the world through their fantasy and heroic play.

ENGAGE!

Parents do not have enough time in the day to dive deep into every fantasy or science fiction interest your child has. It might seem overwhelming to read the entire *Lord of the Rings* series, or watch all of the *Harry Potter* movies in a row, all with the intention to have an engaging conversation, and your instinct would be correct. The best way to start engaging is to ask a few preliminary questions and then dive in with your child.

Instead of reading books alone, make the *Lord of the Rings* books bedtime stories. Play a video game like *Skyrim* or *Legend of Zelda: Breath of the Wild* together, and ask questions about the fantasy elements. Watch a *Harry Potter* movie together once a week. It is not necessary to know every detail about every geek culture story to start relating to our kids.

Pick an interest your child already has and foster it with them. If they love a superhero like the Green Lantern or Aquaman, let them dress up in their costume and explore what it means to behave as their hero. Ask them questions about how their hero would handle everyday chores like homework, dishes, or cleaning their room.

Would the Justice League let Aquaman save the world with them if they couldn't even depend on him to empty the garbage?

Your children can use their hero's exaggerated or supernatural abilities to pursue avenues of imagination that may not be based in reality, but have real influence on their perception of the world. They can mimic many fantasy characters' sense of responsibility to others to incorporate empathy in their play.

You can also engage your child in your geeky interests from when you were young. I introduced my son to *Pokémon* because I had fond memories of its impact on me as a child. Maybe you can propose a *Star Wars* marathon if you watched the original trilogy growing up. Ask your child what they like about the movies, and see if they have a similar interest they can show you next. This kind of back-and-forth sharing can foster strong bonds and a trusting relationship.

Grasping a basic understanding of fantasy, science fiction, and how they are similar and different is the first step in recognizing patterns in geek culture. There are a plethora of genres to explore. Western geek culture usually operates in one of the two genres in this chapter, but in the next chapter, we are going to explore a geek culture medium that bounces between fantasy, science fiction, mystery, thriller, romance, action adventure, and pretty much every other genre of fiction.

CHAPTER 8

THE POWER OF ANIME

"If you don't take risks, you can't create a future!"
— Monkey D. Luffy, One Piece

Some movies make us cry every time we watch them. Maybe your tear-jerker is a soft, animal drama like *Marley & Me*, or a classic like *Old Yeller*. Perhaps you secretly swipe a tissue across your cheek at the end of *Titanic*. There are some films and TV shows out there capable of evoking such powerful emotions that we cannot hold them back. Who can resist ugly crying during the final scene in *The Notebook*?

While we have all experienced the impulse to cry (or try our best not to cry) at powerfully sad or inspiring stories, I would be willing to wager no one has seen a movie or TV show so powerful, it inspired a transcontinental voyage to Antarctica.

Well, no one except Logic Watanabe.

Watanabe watched *A Place Further Than the Universe*, an anime series about a high school girl and her three friends who travel to Antarctica to find her missing mother, who was an Antarctic observation crew member who disappeared on her last expedition.[29] Although many fans of the show credited its moving storyline and engaging characters for their love, Watanabe felt a little stronger about *A Place Further Than the Universe's* emotional impact.

"The aspirations of these girls as they strove to reach Antarctica made me cry, laugh, and think," Watanabe explained in a column about his experience with the series, "After I had watched

---

[29] K, Ben (2019, Feb 6). Anime fan is now reporting from Antarctica, furthest anime pilgrimage site on Earth. Retrieved December 16th, 2021, from http://grapee.jp.

the final episode...utterly overcome as I was with a profound sense of loss, the next thought which entered my mind was: 'I want to go on a pilgrimage to Antarctica.'"

So, he did.

Watanabe scrounged up the cash (about 2 million yen, or 17,600 USD) required for a two-week pilgrimage to Antarctica. He boarded cars, planes, and boats to finally set foot in the setting of his favorite anime series. He broadcasted his experience through Twitter, posting photos of the icy tundra as he explored. He even brought small, cutout figurines of the four girls from *A Place Further than the Universe* and posed them in front of icebergs, frozen tundras, and several penguin gatherings.

Logic Watanabe was moved by the emotional journey of the series' characters, and he felt motivated to explore the world in which he lives. He never would have experienced such a life-changing journey if he had not been so touched. Although few anime fans have picked up and traveled to one of the most unforgiving and remote locations on the planet, there have been others who were similarly moved by the wondrous characters, themes, and stories of Japanese anime.

What makes anime so much more powerful than other animated shows? How is it different from the Western cartoons like *The Flintstones* and *Scooby Doo*? If we as parents want to use elements commonly found in anime to relate to our children, we must first look at the history of the genre and how it has evolved since its inception in 17th century Japan.

ANIME 101

Anime is a style of Japanese animation derived from manga, a Japanese comic book style that heavily features uniquely Eastern illustrations. Unlike American comic books, manga panels are read from right to left. Manga and anime are both part of Japan's visual culture, which relies on vibrant imagery instead of aesthetic values like nonverbal persuasion.

To discover what anime is and how it became popular in Western geek culture, we must first look into the origins of manga. Manga was born out of a desire from the Japanese people to experience **catharsis**, a relieving of emotional tension or purging of emotion.[30] The first instance of manga appeared in 1814 during Japan's Tempo period as a form of caricaturization. This was a dark time in Japanese history—people were starving, scared, and isolated under an oppressive feudal rule. During this time, Katsushika Hokasai, a Japanese artist, released twelve volumes of "random drawings" as a form of catharsis. His drawings featured beautiful women, samurai warriors, urban merchants, and other representations of simpler, more hopeful times in Japanese culture. It struck a powerful chord with everyone who read it.

Manga by design exists to provide therapeutic catharsis to its readers. Hokosai's manga resonated deeply with the people in Japan. The simple drawings validated their feelings by giving them a medium for expression and hope for a brighter future. When the Tempo period ended and life in Japan settled down, the manga still provided readers with a nostalgic glimpse at simpler times.

When Japan opened their trading ports to the US in 1853, this allowed for the first large-scale cultural exchange between the two countries. Western and Eastern visual styles influenced each other in small ways, but manga was not yet as popular as it is today. Most manga created during this time was war propaganda, especially after Japan declared war on the US. Manga resurfaced as a form of therapeutic catharsis after 1945 as a result of the Hiroshima and Nagasaki bombings.

---

[30] Bylsma, L. "When is crying cathartic? An international study." Journal of Social and Clinical Psychology, Vol. 27, No. 10, 2008, pp. 1165-1187

Hiroshima and Nagasaki were decimated by US bombings. Japan's proud culture felt a devastating defeat surge through their nation. The country also experienced a massive influx of orphans, homeless, and sick, poisoned by atom bomb radiation. The country's population felt arguably more hopeless than ever. It was out of this hopelessness that a new era of Japanese art emerged.

Toei Animation, the first large anime company, was founded in 1948 to "give kids hope after the war," according to its current chairman Koei.[31] The reintroduction of manga and anime into Japanese culture once again gave the Japanese an outlet for emotional expression and hope to build back better after the devastation they experienced.

Anime first appeared in the US in 1963, twenty years after the bombings of Nagasaki and Hiroshima, through *AstroBoy*. The cultural import only grew from there: *Speed Racer*, *Dragonball*, and *Mobile Suit Gundam* arrived in the 80s. The rise of Studio Ghibli also began in the 80s, which has since gifted the world with gorgeous animated features like Spirited Away, *Princess Mononoke*, and *Howl's Moving Castle*. Studio Ghibli films tend to be classified in their own sub-genre of anime, but their influence on the culture is undeniable.

After the 80s, mainstream anime viewing appeared through the Toonami channel in the 90s. Where previously kids and teens had to buy or rent anime from their local Blockbuster, on this TV channel they had unprecedented access to anime. The original Toonami lineup combined anime like *Sailor Moon* with Western animated shows like *Thundercat*. It did not take long for Toonami to fill its schedule with a larger variety of anime shows as their popularity in the US soared. This paved the way for the success of shows like *Pokémon, Yu-Gi-Oh*, and *Digimon*, which introduced new anime-inspired games to Western culture.

---

[31] Macwilliams, M. W. (2008). Japanese visual culture: Explorations in the world of manga and anime. Armonk, N.Y.: M.E. Sharpe

The history of manga and anime is important to note because it was, from its inception, a form of catharsis. Anime has continued to be designed for emotional expression; it exists to provide hope to its viewers and inspire them to improve their personal environment through perseverance and resilience. Manga and anime provide their fans with interesting characters and relatable stories through powerful imagery. The predominantly positive messages in manga and anime are what make it so special to fans of the mediums.

ANIME AS A SUBCULTURE

Manga and anime fans discuss their engagement through two terms: fanship and fandoms. **Fanship** describes a fan's level of interest, both emotionally and as an aspect of their identities. High-level fanships might write fan fiction for their favorite animes. **Fandoms** are the communities that connect to, and identify with, each other through their shared fanship.

Although anime was designed to be cathartic specifically for Japanese citizens, US fandoms experienced similar benefits. Most popular US cartoons in the 90s and early 2000s—*The Simpsons*, *Spongebob*, and *Scooby Doo*—were shows with interesting characters and vivid imagery, but no character growth extended outside of any individual episode. Bart Simpson is the same age in 2021 as he was in the first episode from 1989. The Mystery Gang is still made up of the same characters with the same crime-solving skills they had fifty years ago. Unlike the popular Western cartoons, Eastern anime allowed viewers to experience the emotional and physical growth of their favorite characters with each new episode.

Anime characters traditionally begin their journey with profound losses, like the sudden death of a parent or an excommunication from their community. This trope harkens back to the feelings of hopelessness many Japanese citizens felt when anime first entered their society. Throughout the anime's story, these characters must cope with their loss and grow into strong, capable, and emotionally mature beings. Their growth allows them to overcome their grief and find a new home in the world. Anime characters' experiences model the human experience more than Spongebob's stagnant arc, which makes them more relatable for audiences.

Anime has become prevalent in American pop culture within the past decade. The Internet and social media have made cultural exchange easier than ever. Manga, anime, and even American comic books are still viewed as predominantly geek interests in the west, but in Japan, manga and anime are multi-billion dollar industries for all ages to enjoy. Japan's expansive variety of age-appropriate material, genres, and storylines are still laying the groundwork for American culture to explore new forms of anime. Anime is only going to grow in popularity as its relatability grows.

You might recognize some of the most popular animes in America from this book or from your childhood—*Pokémon*, *Sailor Moon*, *Avatar: The Last Airbender*, and InuYasha were often part of Saturday morning cartoon lineups. Shows like *My Hero Academia* and *Demon Slayer* are popular with kids at the time this book is written. While these shows are bright and exciting for young eyes, a cursory glance might throw up some red flags for parents unfamiliar with anime.

ANIME'S MORAL PANIC

If we walked into our living room and saw our kids watching blood gush out of an old man's nose like a broken fire hydrant, our first instinct would probably be to dive toward the television's

OFF button. However, if we knew more about anime's illustrative style, we might be more inclined to let them watch. (Or turn the TV off for a different reason—nosebleeds in anime are a trope that signifies arousal.)

Many parents worry that all anime is violent, sexual, or otherwise inappropriate for their children. The fear that anime might corrupt young minds is yet another moral panic substantiated through parenting sites and news outlets that fundamentally misunderstand anime. As we discussed above, anime's primary function is to promote hopeful imagery and provide catharsis to its viewers. There are anime shows for all different ages, so while some may be too mature for children, there is plenty of age-appropriate anime out there.

Casual violence *does* exist in anime, but no more than classic cartoons like *Tom and Jerry* or Disney's classic Goofy shorts. Tom and Jerry beat each other black and blue in every episode—the cartoon is courteous enough to omit the blood from scenes where Jerry chops off Tom's tail or Tom is brutally mauled by his neighbor's bulldog, Spike. Western animation might be hesitant to display any kind of red liquid alongside their cartoons' antics, but the violence is as real as Eastern depictions in anime.

Violence in cartoons or other forms of geek culture does not promote violence in children. If Popeye could not convince kids across America to pop a can of spinach when they needed a strength boost, anime won't convince them to resort to punching their friends during an argument.[32] The level of violence in anime varies, and as long as your child is watching anime with appropriate ratings, they are not at risk of consuming any dangerous content.

Age appropriate ratings also protect children from viewing any *ecchi* or *hentai* anime, which are more risque shows that fea-

---

[32] Gulati, Vansh. "Is Watching Anime Bad for The Children? – Breaking the Myths!" Epic Dope. Epic Dope, April 26, 2021. https://www.epicdope.com/is-watching-anime-dangerous-is-it-okay-for-children/.

ture partial or full nudity and sexually explicit content. Contrary to what some parents believe, not all anime is sexual in nature. Sexualized anime exists in its own genre, like *Fifty Shades of Grey* exists in a genre separate from *Twilight*. Classifying all anime as illustrated pornography prevents us from exploring the deeply emotional, empowering lessons offered by the majority of anime.

FRIENDSHIP, EFFORT, AND VICTORY

Anime is a special form of entertainment for children because of its relatable characters, unique storylines, and cathartic expressions. Anime serves as a window into Japanese culture while resonating with American audiences in different, albeit equally important ways. Anime has unique archetypes and tropes not found as often in Western stories and characters. Parents and clinicians can draw from these new resources to understand ourselves, our children, and how we relate to others.

There are three important values that the anime medium explores through its characters and stories: friendship, effort, and victory. (This also happens to be the slogan of *Weekly Shonen Jump*, a manga publication.) Almost every anime protagonist begins with a profound loss, and must lean on meaningful connections with friends to recover. Their friends give them a sense of belongingness, self-worth, and acknowledgement. Anime characters often gain their friends as they work together toward a common goal.

Anime series usually set up the main character's goal early in the series: Eren Jaeger wants revenge on the Titans who took his mother in *Attack on Titan*, Tanjiro Kamado wants to save his sister's soul in *Demon Slayer*, and Edward Elric wants to reclaim his brother's human body in *Fullmetal Alchemist: Brotherhood*. The series then follows their journey toward their goal.

The protagonists do not win every time—in fact, they fail often—but in their failures, we see themes of persistence, resilience, integrity, and strength. Eren goes from a young, frightened boy to a fierce, indestructible Titan capable of toppling the government. Edward trades his ability to perform alchemy to retrieve his brother's body and lives happily ever after with his love interest and his brother by his side. When *Demon Slayer's* series finale airs, we can safely assume it will show Tanjiro's efforts rewarded. We resonate with anime heroes' efforts, and when they see victory, it feels more earned than if they had simply tumbled downhill in the general direction of success.

With few exceptions, anime series end with the main character succeeding at their goal and emerging from an epic battle, victorious. Their friends cheer by their side, and while everyone must reflect on the losses along the way, they are grateful overall. The great victory at the conclusion of an anime series gives the protagonist self-acceptance and external validation, leaving viewers with a sense of achievement that can translate into our own lives.

Friendship, effort, and victory are not foreign concepts to most people, but their applications in the real world can be difficult to achieve. Friends come and go. Effort sometimes goes unrewarded. Victory is not always guaranteed. Conversely, in anime, these concepts are constants, which proves to be reassuring for audiences and makes them feel like no matter what happens in their own lives, they can turn to anime for reminders that these three pillars are unshakeable.

Themes of friendship, effort, and victory are not the only parts of anime resonating with audiences. With such a wide variety of anime out there, it is unsurprising that most viewers find a connection to some of the characters. They remind us of ourselves, whether they exemplify traits we have or traits we *feel* we have. Many of my clients resonate with the main characters in anime who have lost or been abandoned by their family, even if they are coming from a relatively healthy home, because they *feel* just as alone.

Remember Lucy from Chapter One? Her favorite character in the anime series *Bungo Stray Dogs* was the protagonist, Atsushi Nakajima. He was an outcast, misunderstood by the staff at his orphanage so severely they threw him out on the street. Lucy still lived at home with her mother, but Atsushi's quest to find a reason to live after being abandoned resonated with her. She felt just as alone, afraid, and hopeless as Atsushi felt at the beginning of the anime series. Her emotional connection to the character enticed her to keep watching. Lucy felt like *Bungo Stray Dogs* could be telling her story in a more narrative form.

I watched hours of *Bungo Stray Dogs* so I could understand how Lucy felt. We talked together about her feelings of isolation and what it meant for her to feel like no one related to her through Atsushi's lens. We were able to explore *why* she related to Atsushi, and how we can become a better version of the character trope. If Lucy was going to embody friendship, effort, and victory, we had to figure out what they looked like for her.

Lucy's mother, when she first came to me, believed anime was the root of Lucy's mental health trouble. She believed her daughter was locking herself away in a fantasy world so she could avoid facing hardships and connecting with others. She wanted me to tell Lucy to stop watching anime altogether. Lucy's mom did not understand how taking anime away from her daughter would remove the only thing keeping her from slipping over the edge.

Instead of removing anime from her life, I told Lucy's mom we were going to relate to her through an interest she already had established. As her mom started watching *Cowboy Bebop* with her, Lucy developed trust with her mother and started opening up about her life. Their bond formed through the relatable characters present throughout anime. Lucy developed a friendship with her mother through a shared interest, and started putting effort into their relationship. Her hard work to be seen and understand others allowed Lucy to fully recover, victorious.

Lucy found herself in an isolated protagonist, but this is only one of many tropes people identify with in anime stories. There are other tropes we can relate to our children as they uncover new situations in their lives. For example, a "tsundere" is a character in anime who starts their relationship with a love interest cold and hard, but softens up and comes around as the story progresses. This is another great trope to explore when a young man or woman is struggling with their feelings for a peer for the first time. We can use common character tropes to understand ourselves and the people around us better because they are based on common types of people found in the real world.

We can combine anime character tropes with storylines to engage with our children on deeper levels. Hope, resilience, meaningful relationships, and victory are all essential components of anime storylines. These stories are built to be emotionally powerful to allow catharsis for the audience. The audience cries when a beloved character dies, and laughs at the adventuring party's antics. Anime stories touch our soul by design and give us an outlet to express our emotions.

It might not sound like crying over an animated character with your child is the best way to engage them, but studies have proved the opposite. Crying with another person has been shown to promote bonding when both parties are crying over a shared experience. Crying in front of someone who is also crying can make one feel their emotions are a valid and reasonable response.[33] We can share our tears with our children and to signal emotional expression as normal, valid, and acceptable as a form of catharsis.

---

[33] Tel Aviv University. "Why Cry? Evolutionary Biologists Show Crying Can Strengthen Relationships." ScienceDaily. www.sciencedaily.com/releases/2009/08/090824141045.htm (accessed December 14, 2021).

The caveat to these studies is that displays of catharsis vary in appropriateness between cultures. American culture is extremely low-context, meaning we often express our emotions either verbally or physically. Crying in front of another American is more likely to promote a bond. Japanese culture is high-context, meaning thoughts and feelings are expressed indirectly. People in Japan may be more reluctant to overtly express a sensitive emotion like crying.

If this is the case, why is everyone in anime expressing their emotions in melodramatic ways?

THE PRACTICAL FUNCTIONS OF ANIME

There is a higher non-verbal and contextual load on communicators in Japanese culture than we experience in America. Since anime operates as a form of catharsis primarily for Japanese viewers, the animation style uses **cathartic expressions** to convey the characters' emotions. Cathartic expressions are exaggerated, overproduced facial expressions and body movements to make what the characters are feeling apparent to the audience.

If the eyes are the window to the soul, the reason anime characters have big eyes is to easily express their most precious feelings. Happy characters have big sparkles in their eyes. Angry characters have scrunched up faces and cruciforms on their foreheads. Drops of sweat appear on the foreheads of stressed or confused characters. Cathartic expressions give Japanese audiences a break from determining other people's emotions all day.

Other animation techniques in anime also signal what the onscreen characters are feeling. Most background colors align with the feelings of the characters in the scene—pink, sparkly backgrounds denote happiness and romantic feelings while blues and purples depict despair or hopelessness. Anime tries to make it easy for audiences to determine characters' emotions so they can focus on other story elements.

Cathartic expressions and color palettes in anime can help developing children contextualize what different feelings look like. Children who watch anime often will begin to understand that tears are sad, goofy grins are happy, and furrowed brows are angry. Adding colored backgrounds to these emotions help children understand color's association with emotions at a younger age than they would without watching anime.

Anime acts as a window into Japanese culture, where the people do not explicitly share every thought and feeling, but actively try to work out what is going on inside the mind of their neighbor. Japan has a collectivist culture, which relies on the community to anticipate each other's needs. Group harmony is valued higher than individual expression of opinions in Japan. People immersed in Japanese culture are more likely to show loyalty to their extended family and community than their American counterparts.

The US is more individualistic, meaning most people who grew up with US culture expect others to fend for themselves. Americans are more likely to show loyalty only to their immediate families and value their independence over deeper relationships with others in their community. Americans' worth is often based on merit, as opposed to personality-based merit found in more collectivist societies.

Anime often explores the difference between the two culture types. Some characters in anime begin with individualistic goals that are put on hold by a more pressing, collectivist mission. Kaneki Ken wanted to find a girlfriend in *Tokyo Ghoul* and stopped his search to protect the other characters from danger. Eren, Mikasa, and Armin wanted to travel the world in *Attack on Titan*, but tragedy and a sense of duty redirected them into the

Survey Corps to protect their community from imminent danger. By placing individualist and collectivist values in direct conflict, anime often creates a struggle that both American and Japanese audiences can identify in their own lives.

The way the character anticipates the wants, needs, and feelings of their friends is an example of a collective culture thought process. Anime characters frequently deliver internal monologues to the audience, explaining their thought process while they figure out how the other members of their party might feel if they stole an extra piece of bread from the rations or ran off in the night alone to face the Big Bad Guy. They anticipate the reactions of others, and if they determine their actions will damage their party's opinion of them, most characters choose to stay put, because their self-worth comes from the value their friends place in them.

Anime is a more friend and family-centric genre because of the influence from Japan's collective culture. However, in Western culture's TV shows, characters often abandon their party to accomplish a task, which enforces an individualistic mentality. Western horror movies indulge in this trope even though they know the audience is screaming, *"Don't split up! Why would you do that?"* at their TVs. In *The Incredibles* movie, Mr. Incredible leaves his family to fight crime in secret and takes a new superjob without telling his wife, despite the fact that she (and their children) are also superheroes. He places his own self-worth above his safety, despite how his family would feel if he ran into trouble on one of his secret missions. (Spoiler alert—he does.)

Exposing ourselves and our children to anime can help us learn empathy and communication skills commonly inferred in collective cultures. In *Cowboy Bebop*, a science fiction anime about intergalactic bounty hunters, the original group members on Spaceship Bebop are quirky and ineffective on their own. Spike is a fugitive, Faye is an amnesiac con artist, and Ein...is a corgi. Although each character is a misfit by themselves, they come together to form a powerful, unstoppable team. Their shared experiences foster love, acceptance, forgiveness, and respect for one another.

The Spaceship Bebop crew forms a collective and works together well throughout the series. Each character learns to subvert their weaknesses and showcase their strengths through their teammates, which is a valuable skill for our children to learn.

Teamwork displayed in anime series can also promote positive self-identity. When we relate to a team member in an anime, we are encouraged to feel like we matter to others the same way Spike matters to Jet in *Cowboy Bebop*. Most anime series feature similar ragtag groups of adventurers who teach children and adults their individual value through group cooperation. Luffy has his Straw Hat Pirates in *One Piece*, the Elric brothers gather a small team throughout *Fullmetal Alchemist: Brotherhood*, and the Sailor Scouts collectively fight against evil in *Sailor Moon*. As anime teaches us how powerful we can be when we are bolstered by people who care about us, we discover our individual power as well.

We can use anime's lessons about personal power to encourage our neurodivergent children to understand their diagnoses as a unique part of them. Characters displayed with traits commonly found in neurodivergent people can help them overcome negative impressions of neurodivergence. These characters may be different, but they still make friends, put in effort, and find victory on their journey.

A common theme in anime is that the most exceptional characters fall outside of what society deems as "normal." Naruto is an anime protagonist who displays some traits commonly viewed as negative symptoms of ADHD: he is disorganized, loud, struggles with didactic work, and struggles to focus on some of his more arduous tasks while he trains to become a ninja. However, Naruto excels at hands-on tasks and can work harder and longer than his peers. Traditional problem-solving vexes him, but he often thinks outside of the box and handles situations from creative angles. Naruto is fiercely determined and persistent in his efforts to grow and improve. We can bring attention to Naruto's positive traits, letting our children know their diagnosis is not a hindrance, it just needs to be viewed from different angles.

Shinji Ikari from *Neon Genesis: Evangelion* struggles with anxiety and depression throughout the series. He has a duty to protect the world and do his job, but his depression makes it difficult for him to complete tasks. Shinji struggles with his deteriorating self-worth throughout the series. At the series' infamously figurative ending, Shinji comes to terms with his depression and discovers how meaningful his life is through his shared existence with other people. Children and adults with depression can look at Shinji's struggle and identify with him. He makes them feel like they matter, and like their diagnosis won't prevent them from making progress.

By exploring the characters viewed as "abnormal" in Western TV series, we can help children who struggle with their diagnoses see how they can still make lasting friendships, persist through hardships, and emerge victorious.

ENGAGING WITH YOUR CHILD

Watching anime with your child for the first time might feel a little like diving headfirst into cold water. It might come with an initial shock, but once you get used to the cathartic expressions and exaggerated verbal cues, you will be able to more easily absorb the cultural differences between anime and Western animation. You also have some cool background information on the origins of anime to share with your child.

There are two different ways to listen to anime while you watch, and depending on which your child prefers, your experience may differ. **Subbed** anime viewing involves watching the show with its original Japanese voice actors and English (or another native language) subtitles. **Dubbed** refers to voice-dubbing, where actors reenact the characters post-production in their native language, like English, Spanish, or French. There are pros and cons to each method: reading subs while absorbing animated action can be overwhelming, while dubs usually feature clunkier voice acting than traditional Japanese audio. The choice between the two methods comes down to personal preference.

Although the shift into a new style of storytelling might be shocking at first, anime quickly reels you in with its complex characters and stakes-heavy storylines. Once you've got a grasp on the common tropes and story flow in anime, you will probably enjoy it more than you expected. Maybe you will even find a character with traits you recognize in yourself or your child. Even if one anime story does not pique your interest, there are plenty to try. Anime is becoming more popular and can be found on platforms like Netflix, Hulu, Funimation, and practically any other streaming service out there today.

Some parents prefer lighthearted anime like *My Neighbor Totoro* and *Spirited Away* from Studio Ghibli. Some immediately invest in romance anime series like *Kane Karo*. A great way to get started is to try out a genre you know you enjoy from other fiction works. You might be more familiar with an anime series' overarching themes and beats when you have a working knowledge of the genre's tropes in Western fiction.

Once the two of you have watched a few episodes of anime together, talk to your child about what you like and dislike about anime. Ask them if there is a character they feel connected to, or if there is a character they cannot stand. Some kids immediately take to Naruto, while others side with his rival, Sasuke, and think Naruto is obnoxious and arrogant. Anime was designed to help us better understand the world we live in and how it can improve, so conversations around anime themes are easy ways to engage with our children.

Engaging with our kids does not have to be all psychoanalysis and no play—we can also discuss the show with them simply because we are interested! Anime is meant to be cathartic, but it is also meant to be *fun*. Talk about your theories for upcoming episodes together. Pick your favorite character pairing and write fanfic for them. Ask questions about what anime you should watch together next. Generate excitement with your kid—you have a new shared experience! Now you have an entertaining, engaging pastime to share, and you have new insight into what is most important to your child during their own hero's journey.

CHAPTER 9

COMIC BOOKS & SUPERHEROES

"Comic books to me are fairy tales for grown-ups."
— Stan Lee

As parents, we secretly hope our children see us as their own personal heroes. We sacrifice our time, money, and sanity for our kids, and we do our best to protect them from evil. Parenting *is* heroic, even though the job does not come with its own set of superpowers. We only hope our children look past our normal strength and non-laser-eyes to see SuperMom and DynoDad anyways. Unfortunately, few of us are privy to that special recognition.

When I asked a client, Andy, to build his own superhero comic book, he did not base his hero on his mom or dad. He built a superhero named Chicken Nugget Man. Chicken Nugget Man defeated all the villains he faced by force-feeding them chicken nuggets until they surrendered.

I told him although chicken nuggets are delicious, I was not confident his hero would emerge victorious from *every* battle with an evil villain. Andy was adamant Chicken Nugget Man would always be there to save the day. I worried he was not taking the assignment seriously, but pressed forward with my plan.

It turned out, a superhero always available to provide comfort food and some light humor was more important to Andy than he initially thought. Andy was stuck in the middle of his parents' nasty divorce. His life was in a period of transition and he felt neglected, guilty, and insecure. His superhero story helped him explore his emotions from a safe distance. We built Andy's comic book to explore Chicken Nugget Man's goals, persona, and sense of identity. By the time we were ready to "send it off for print," Andy made an amazing discovery about his personal superhero: not only was Chicken Nugget Man a hero to Andy, he was also the hero Andy wanted to *be*.

The lack of stability in Andy's situation made him want to provide for others experiencing similar struggles. Chicken nuggets are a comfort food for a boy his age: easy to make, easy to eat, easy to share. Chicken Nugget Man allowed Andy to rewrite his own story and explore different obstacles in his life from a safely imagined, heroic perspective.

Comic books are valuable tools for developing minds like Andy's because they encourage their readers to resonate with their adventures. By examining the place of superheroes in geek culture, we can see how super quests touch the hearts of many young boys and girls all over the world. We can even relate these quests back to our personal journeys as parents, discovering our own goals, outlooks on life, and even our own weaknesses. Before extrapolating valuable lessons from the superhero genre, we must explore the history of superheroes. Much like superhero origin stories supply us with vital information about the boundaries, strengths, and weaknesses of the heroes, comic books' origin story reveals some much needed context for how the genre can be beneficial for our children.

THE ORIGIN STORY: FROM DIMES TO CRIMES

Many superhero fans consider Superman the first superhero. When many adults first think of superheroes, they might recall his jingle from the 1941 television show or other adaptations since:

> *Faster than a speeding bullet,*
> *More powerful than a locomotive,*
> *Able to leap tall buildings in a single bound,*
> *The infant of Krypton is now the Man of Steel…*
> *Superman!*

Although heroes like the Phantom, Ogon Bat, and Mandrake the Magician predate Superman's debut in 1938, Superman popularized superheroes and arguably defined the trope for future use: costume, codename, superhuman abilities, and a selfless mission. After Superman's initial success, a boom of superheroes landed on the scene through the same medium: comic books. Batman, Wonder Woman, and Captain America quickly made an impression on popular culture through dime comics. From *Action Comics* #1 in 1938 to the early 1950s, these heroes maintained what many comic book fans consider the "Golden Age" of comics. It was during this time superheroes found their way into the hearts of so many Americans.

In the beginning of the Golden Age, America was faced with the difficult decision of whether to join World War II. National anxiety grew as we struggled to come to terms with the state of our world. Much like the effect anime had during the Tempo period in Japan, superhero stories provided hope and catharsis for audiences in America. In these stories, fictional super threats were challenged by super humans, and the threats were defeated by truth, justice, and altruism.

Superman often fought exaggerated versions of whatever plagued society at the time of their stories' publishings. Superman triumphed over Adolf Hitler and Joseph Stalin in his 1940s comics. In the 1950s, he investigated new radioactive threats and those "pesky Communists" while Americans lived through the Cold War and the Red scare. He is the embodiment of perseverance and resilience, and people loved him because he triumphed over any and all issues his audience perceived as insurmountable.

Although Superman's adaptability served his character well at first, many found it difficult to relate to the all-powerful being. Superman did not work for his powers, he was born with them. His list of abilities is seemingly endless: super strength, invulnerable skin, super speed, flight, X-Ray vision, heat vision, super hearing, freeze breath... and his only weakness comes in the form of a mysterious rock called Kryptonite. When World War II ended and tensions faded in America, people had trouble resonating with characters like Superman. How are we, as human beings, supposed to relate to someone whose only weakness is an alien rock?

Most heroes during the Golden Age had a vast variety of powers and notably few vulnerabilities. In the wake of World War II, though, superheroes' popularity began to dwindle and comic book publishers had to explore other genres for business, like comedy, horror, and investigative mysteries. And while our superheroes hung up their capes one at a time, a dangerous threat began closing in on the comic book world...

THE SUPER MORAL PANIC APPEARS

In 1954, psychologist Dr. Frederic Wertham published a book titled *Seduction of the Innocent*.[34] The book vilified comic books as the root cause of juvenile delinquency. He referred to comics as an "injury to the eye" and argued their themes of violence, homosexuality (which was still viewed as a mental disorder at the time), and nudity were corrupting America's youth. Since the comic book industry was still relatively new, it was too unstable to defend against Wertham's outlandish claims, and business fell victim to a full-blown moral panic.

Scholars have since debunked the majority of Wertham's arguments in the book, pointing out how he exaggerated both

---

[34] Wertham, Fredric. 1954. *Seduction of the Innocent*. Rinehart & Company. pp. 192, 234–235.

sample size and substance. Wertham conducted his interviews on young comic book fans with previous records of deviance and falsely determined the correlation as causation. His "research" has been proven to be more creative anecdote than hard evidence. However, at the time *Seduction of the Innocent* hit the shelves in the 1950s, parents across the nation panicked.

Wertham's book rose in popularity and became a minor bestseller as his warnings resonated with parents across the country. He appeared in public and held conferences to defend his position. Religious groups held public comic book burnings to set paper ablaze. Artists and writers abandoned their posts in droves, and comic book shops were driven largely underground. Still, the assault on the new creative industry continued to intensify. In a live television broadcast, U.S. Senator, Estes Kefauver, called the comic book industry "more dangerous than Hitler ever was," which caused an uproar in the media.[35] The calamity grew strong enough to trigger a U.S. Congressional investigation into the comic book industry.

Publishers were already struggling to make ends meet as their superheroes dwindled by the day, and the inquiry did not bode well for the future of comic books. The Association of Comics Magazine Publishers worked to establish the Comics Code Authority (CCA), a form of self-censorship that would prevent government interference in comic book creation.[36] However, the forty-one standards they came up with to appease the government ended up being more stifling than the publishers hoped.

The moral panic devastated the comic book industry. In an attempt to protect their children, most parents had already banned comic books from their homes after hearing about their supposed

---

[35] Abad-Santos, Alex. "The Insane History of How American Paranoia Ruined and Censored Comic Books." Vox. Vox Media, December 15, 2014. https://www.vox.com/2014/12/15/7326605/comic-book-censorship.

[36] Eury, M., Misiroglu, G., & Sanderson, P. (2017, February 1). *Superheroes: World War II*. Encyclopædia Britannica. Retrieved January 4, 2022, from https://www.britannica.com/art/superhero/World-War-II

corrupting effect. Then the CCA prevented comic book publishers from creating any sort of sex, crime, violence, or horror that might appeal to older audiences. Publishers could not see a way to make up the profits they lost by losing their fanbase. The comic book industry appeared to be doomed. The Golden Age appeared to be over.

THE SILVER AGE OF COMICS & THE RETURN OF SUPERHEROES

Only Superman, Wonder Woman, and Batman survived the moral panic of the 1950s. Still, even these heroes suffered from the CCA and struggled to hold the comic book industry afloat. It was not until The Flash appeared in *Showcase* #4 in 1956 that publishers saw a glimmer of hope for their industry's future. From 1956 to 1960, DC's superhero revival with The Flash, Green Lantern, and the Manhunter from Mars paved a way for other comic book publishers, like Marvel and Archie Comics, to capitalize on the resurging market.

By the middle of the 1960s, superheroes were back in full swing. This time around, superheroes were less concerned about existential threats. They were built to model the human experience of their audience. With only one special ability, new superheroes were truly tested by their nemeses. This meant they had to rely on creative problem-solving and quick thinking to save the day. The evolution of superheroes did not stop with their abilities, though.

New and revived heroes were also given full-on personalities to further resonate with readers. Marvel's first Fantastic Four iteration featured a stuffy Mr. Fantastic, a shy Sue Storm, a short-tempered Human Torch, and the grumpy Thing. Each character's unique personality flaw not only hindered their heroic actions, it sometimes acted as a cause for new problems. Marvel Comics continued to create heroes with complex, flawed personalities who explored consequences more grounded in the audience's world.

From the beginning of the Silver Age to modern publications, comic books have served their audiences real-life struggles through fantastical lenses. Today, comic books are finally phasing out of their moral panic and making their way into the heart of mainstream culture. The success of the MCU made a large contribution to repairing the damage done in the late 1950s. Comic books' similarities to other mediums in geek culture are what make them so special, and their success is vital to the heartbeat of the culture as comic books are often the cornerstones on which local game stores—the central hubs of geek culture—are built.

As parents, if we can understand the importance of superheroes and the comic book medium, we can begin to strengthen our relationships with our kids in leaps and bounds. Their colorful graphics, bold texts, and complex heroes teach us about the nuances of life from a safe distance. They allow us to explore endless possibilities in a low-stakes environment, and by tackling impossible scenarios they teach us about our own limitations... as well as our potential.

The colorful personalities of Silver Age heroes throw them into fresh, new situations previously unexplored in the comic book world. Some heroes triumph without fail no matter what is thrown at them, but the heroes with the most recognition today are ones who struggle to balance their altruism with their human nature. The new standards and deviations presented during the Silver Age are best examined through three different types of characters, each exemplifying struggles that make superheroes so valuable today: the Ideal Hero, the Vigilante, and the Atoner.

THE IDEAL HERO: THE AMAZING SPIDER-MAN

Immediately following Marvel's success with the Fantastic Four, writer Stan Lee was encouraged to create another completely original character. He developed a shy, nerdy, high-school orphan who was constantly bullied by his peers. When the boy, Peter Parker, is bitten by a radioactive spider, he gains a few superpowers: the proportional strength of a spider, the ability to climb walls and stick to other surfaces, and a Spider-Sense (or Peter tingle) alerts him to incoming danger. Peter Parker becomes Spider-Man, and although he is young, Spider-Man feels a sense of responsibility to protect his home of New York City from danger.

Peter Parker is known for his snarky comebacks, creative innovation, and resilience in the face of tragedy. He is an underdog hero who worked hard for his job, his secret identity, his super accessories, and still faces hardships capable of crumpling any non-superhero if they experienced *just* one of them. Spider-Man's story begins with the death of his parents and quickly escalates. When Peter Parker makes a quick decision not to stop a crook from rushing past him on the street, the same crook carries on to shoot his Uncle Ben. This initial tragedy threatened to turn Peter into a villain, but instead, it instills a lesson in him, and he makes a vow to act only in ways that protect the people around him.

Spider-Man is arguably Marvel's most successful superhero because he demonstrates many of the character traits audiences identify with or strive to have. Comic book readers want to identify with the heroes, and an ideal hero like Spider-Man makes this connection easy. We celebrate his wins and grieve his losses right alongside him as we read. Reading about Superman moving planets in and out of orbit with his bare hands is exciting once, but we resonate more with heroes who overcome obstacles we can identify as similar to our own—obstacles we cannot overcome with bare fists.

While most superheroes face struggles with brute physical force, Peter Parker is still growing up and has to balance his two contrasting identities. In the same volume we might watch him battle a supervillain or two, but we might also see him fall in love for the first time, grieve the loss of loved ones, and find ways to make rent for his New York City apartment. He has all of the traits of the most beloved superheroes while struggling with the same situations any teenager or young adult has growing up.

Spider-Man is one of the few superheroes who is constantly learning as he goes. After the release of the movie, *Spider-Man: No Way Home*, a fan commented on a message board, "I might be oversimplifying this, but couldn't Peter Parker have avoided this entire story if he just thought about his choices for more than five seconds?"

Another user immediately replied, "You just described every Spider-Man story ever."

Spider-Man's personality traits get him into trouble as often as they get him out. We learn through his character how relying too heavily on *any* skill—especially a super skill—can be dangerous. Peter's reliance on his super skills and ego prove to be a fatal mistake in the controversial comic series *The Amazing Spider-Man #121-122*. In these issues, Peter's nonchalant fighting attitude costs his girlfriend her life.

When the Green Goblin tosses Gwen Stacey off a bridge, Spider-Man shoots a web after her and catches her by the leg. He immediately starts celebrating as he reels her up the bridge toward him, saying,

"Not only am I the most *dashing* hero on two legs—I'm easily the most versatile. Who else could save a falling girl from certain dea—*Gwen?*"

Despite Peter Parker's extensive scientific and mathematical knowledge, he failed to consider how grabbing her by the leg and sharply stopping her fall could hurt her. The abrupt *SNAP* catches Gwen's body, but breaks her neck. Swearing revenge on the Green Goblin, Peter assaults the villain, letting his grief take over and morph into rage. He only stops himself when the Goblin falls unconscious. Peter reflects, saying, "In another moment I might have *killed* him! I would have become like him—a—a *murderer!*" and swings off to calm himself and regain control of his emotions. Eventually, he comes to terms with his own role in Gwen's death. He has to reconcile his love for her with his responsibility to keep her safe. He faces loss *and* failure, and has to find a way to come out the other side.

Spider-Man resonates with people because of his emotional honesty. We do not need to experience an active role in someone's death to understand the complex guilt Peter faces after losing Uncle Ben and Gwen Stacey. Losing a friend is a familiar human experience. Peter might have to deflect a few more missiles than we do, but his emotional experiences are the same ones we go through every day.

Still, despite all Spider-Man has been through, there is never a question of whether he is a hero or a villain. The lines are not blurred for Peter Parker. Even in his darkest moment, he is able to pull himself back from the edge. His sense of responsibility and altruism is only strengthened by the hardships he faces. He is an ideal character to explore personal strength, resilience, and perseverance during tough times. Some heroes in the comic book world struggle more than Spider-Man to maintain emotional stability, but these complicated characters are still helpful for identifying with the human experience.

THE VIGILANTE: BATMAN

Many believe *The Amazing Spider-Man #121-#122* single-handedly ushered in the Bronze Age of comic books—one where superhero stories dive into deeper, darker territory. The shift from good-versus-evil had been gradual before, but when Marvel killed off a beloved character previously considered "untouchable," superheroes across all comic book publishers felt the effects of Gwen's death. One standout example of the new "dark and gritty" superheroes came from the *Batman: The Dark Knight Returns* comic series released in 1986.

Superheroes survived the moral panic by remaining unshakenly "good." When the Bronze Age ushered in a line of superheroes struggling to maintain this image, parental concern returned. Parents may have remembered the goofy, do-gooder Batman from Adam West's portrayal in the 1960s live-action movies, but when their children brought home comics with a dark, menacing vigilante on the cover, they worried about his influence on their young ones' moral compasses. The new Batman struggled with complex topics previously unheard of for superheroes, and although they were "darker" than his classic detective cases of the past, his character complexity was exactly what made him one of the world's most popular superheroes.

Superheroes (and super villains) who explore moral ambiguity are more relatable to children. This can be hard for parents to wrap their heads around. We want to believe our kids are *only* capable of doing good in the world, not horrendous evil. However, children who are never shown the choice between good and evil struggle to learn how to make the right choice. Thus, children still learning the difference between good and evil, right and wrong, are especially affected by the stories told in Bronze Age comics. Morally ambiguous characters make us confront our understanding of these concepts and determine where we lie on the spectrum in our own life. It can be uncomfortable to see "heroes" make questionable decisions, but as comic book stories explore virtue conflicts, we are forced to reconcile with our own moral code.

Batman, unlike Spider-Man, does not observe a solid line between good and evil. His motives are less altruistic than those of the Ideal Heroes of his time. This placed him in a new category of superheroes: the Vigilante. Batman is a complicated character torn up by grief and vengeance. When Bruce Wayne, Batman's secret identity, lost his parents as a child, he swore to avenge them and take down every criminal in Gotham City. His entire personality is built upon the trauma he suffered on that one fateful night. He often acts on impulse, and although he upholds the common heroic trope of never killing his targets, he often beats and tortures them in the name of justice.

Batman does not view himself as a hero at all, and often refers to himself as "the night" or "vengeance." He is unafraid to break laws to achieve his goals. This may be reason enough for most parents to avoid Batman. However, Batman's complicated relationships with good and evil make him an even more relatable character than some Ideal Heroes. Making the "right" decision is a universally difficult part of the human experience, and it is one Batman struggles with often. Most Batman stories take place when Bruce Wayne is a middle-aged man, which makes it even more interesting when he realizes he does not have all the answers. He is a case study of how tragedy can affect a person in their adult life, which was not a commonly explored concept until Batman's experiences appeared in comic book shops.

Batman fans might not all be orphans, but most can identify with his overwhelming loss and grief. Most children have been "orphaned" in some way: maybe they have been kicked off a sports team, or lost their social circle and experienced the orphaned "essence." Batman provides representation for feelings of loneliness, mistrust after betrayal, and isolation, which are all concepts children—and young adults, especially—struggle to understand on their own. His character, though flawed, gives his audience a harmonization of those archetypal feelings.

Some parents may find Batman comics disturbing. He does have some pretty intense series, including *The Long Halloween*, *The Killing Joke*, and *Death of the Family*. Sometimes Batman deals with sexually explicit situations, abuse, psychological torture, and brutal loss. The darker and grittier content may shock parents at first. It is imperative to recognize, though, that although these concepts are intended for more mature readers, they are the setting of the story.

Settings exist as precursors for the hero to come in and rectify. If all comic books dealt with PG-rated settings, we would pretty quickly burn out on repetitive and unrealistic stakes. Exploring mature content in superhero stories does not mean our children will read them and think, "Well, maybe I should do that." Exposure does not imply impersonation. Playing Monopoly does not make anyone a millionaire. Watching a nature documentary is not granting anyone the title of explorer. *Better Homes & Gardens* readers are not automatically considered designers. We are exposed to all kinds of information with no influence on us on a daily basis, and stories about Batman saving the city from absolutely insane criminals is no different.

Comic book stories give us metaphorical examples of what we are feeling and where those feelings could take us. Spider-Man may be a hero who takes the high road whenever possible, regardless of his feelings, but Batman sometimes slips from hero status as he tries to exact his revenge on the criminal underworld of Gotham City. While no one in the real world experiences superhuman abilities, we *do* experience varying weights of responsibility, temptation to act recklessly, and difficulty reconciling our sense of identity. Vigilante superheroes provide a lens through which we can examine these real questions from a safe distance.

Technically, all superheroes are vigilantes from a legal standpoint. However, Batman and other heroes who struggle to balance good intentions with actions often deviate from the superhero "moral code" we came to understand through Ideal Heroes. It is important to understand this distinction before examining the third archetype of superheroes, and it is the most complicated of the three: the Atoner.

THE ATONER: THE WINTER SOLDIER

Redemption arcs are some of the most popular stories in modern culture. We love to see a character at their worst realize their mistakes, dust themselves off, and try to make it right. The concept is relatable; we have all given the kids a few extra minutes before bed because we felt bad about yelling at them earlier. Giving them a reward to make up for our bad actions makes us feel like we have made up for our mistake, even if we did not explicitly apologize. While most superheroes (and other characters) in comic books atone for a mistake at some point in their story, no one embodies the experience of atonement as well as James Buchanan "Bucky" Barnes, aka The Winter Soldier.

Bucky Barnes begins his hero career as a sidekick to Captain America, but when a mission goes wrong and both heroes are assumed dead, Cap is frozen in ice and Bucky is nowhere to be found. We later discover that Bucky Barnes lost his memory and was captured by the enemy. They brainwashed him into becoming their Winter Soldier: a ruthless, covert assassin, committing violent atrocities against the people with whom he used to serve. After Bucky finally regains his memories after years of brutality, he spends all of his time atoning for his actions.

Bucky's experiences leave him distrustful of others and himself. He is always waiting for his memory to betray him and send him back down into a murderous rampage. He is confident anyone close to him will realize how abhorrent he is and leave him behind.

Although he spends his time trying to atone for his mistakes, his actions do not remove the guilt lurking inside of him.

We do not see Bucky fully earn his redemption until Marvel's TV series, *The Falcon and the Winter Soldier*. Bucky Barnes goes to therapy throughout the series, making him one of the few superheroes to seek professional help for his issues. He expresses his hesitation to commit to therapy several times, but as the show continues, we see him make real progress toward self-acceptance and forgiveness. He learns to cope with his survivor's guilt and trauma. He even makes progress in his interpersonal relationships. Bucky's redemption arc is based in fiction, but his process is based in real, relatable experiences. We can apply some of them to our own lives. We see Bucky's trial-and-error approach to redemption and watch him learn hard lessons so we do not have to make the same mistakes.

Bucky begins his atonement by working alongside the military, taking down the same operatives who kidnapped and brainwashed him. He initially believes this path is the smartest one, but after a time, he realizes he has been enacting revenge instead of seeking redemption. His misguided actions reveal the reason he does not feel any better about himself or his experience. It is not until he starts acting selflessly and confronting the consequences of his actions directly that he begins to know peace.

We as parents can use stories like Bucky's to provide new perspectives to our children. Redemption is a concept they will undoubtedly experience at some point in their life. When they read about it in a comic book or watch it on TV, it makes the process easier to understand. It sets them up for their own redemption process that may come later down the line. Your children can accompany an Atoner down the path of redemption and feel a sense of resonance, empathy, and encouragement they might not get from Batman or Spider-Man. This makes the Atoner an invaluable archetype to have available during the toughest parts of life.

CONNECT, COMMUNICATE, & EVALUATE

Comic books and superheroes contain excellent mythos to explore with our children. They are entertaining because of their bright colors, dramatic stakes, and exciting plots, but they also provide an abundance of life lessons. Take Batman and Robin's dynamic duo roles, for example, and apply them to our own roles as parent and child. It is our responsibility to guide our sidekicks. We train them for difficult decisions in the future. We coach them through identity crises. We feel overwhelming pride when they succeed. Like Batman's various Robin sidekicks, though, our students will inevitably surpass their masters. It is our job to make sure our Robin goes on to become the brave, daring Nighthawk, and not the vindictive, conniving Riddler.

Supervillains have become more compelling than their puppy-stomping, evil-plan-announcing ancestors. While most supervillains in the Bronze Age acted as a foil for their hero, modern versions of villains are more complex. These villains give audiences more engaging opportunities to learn about their own moral structures. Complex villains often have relatable motivations, heart wrenching backstories, and captivating moments of action. Ra's al Ghul and the League of Assassins truly believe they are removing evil from Gotham City in *Batman*, despite their methods involving killing off most of humanity. In *The Avengers: Infinity War*, Thanos' plan to painlessly eliminate half of life in the universe to conserve resources sparked debates online between people who saw him as a villain and those who viewed his endeavor as noble. We learn right from wrong in more nuanced ways when supervillains display complex moral codes and struggle to balance their good and evil sides just like the superheroes they battle.

From the Golden Age of comic books to the Modern Era of the MCU, comic book characters have never been more popular than they are right now. There are a multitude of ways to explore the genre together. There has also been a massive increase in representation in the last decade, which makes room for even more relatability. We have seen live-action representation of women superheroes like the Scarlet Witch and Captain Marvel, minority heroes like Shang-Chi and the Black Panther, and LGBT+ characters represented through Deadpool and Loki (admittedly, his gender fluid identity took a while to appear on screen). Even more diverse characters exist in the world of comic books—there is a story for everyone.

You can take a trip down to your local friendly game store almost any day of the year and browse the comic book shelves with your kid. Some shops can be overwhelming on the first trip. You might not know more than a few members of the Avengers, and you may not fully grasp the difference between DC and Marvel heroes. Comic book shops are often filled to the brim with comic book accessories like art, action figures, and costume pieces. This can immediately distract first-timers from any sense of organization. Even if you find a character who looks interesting to you, it is difficult to pinpoint the beginning of their story after the many reboots, reimaginings, and resurrections comics often put their heroes through. The best way to break past this barrier is to simply grab a comic that looks interesting, and start reading. Eventually, you will find a series you or your child like.

There is no one way to start reading comics. You can always start with one of your kid's favorite series and work your way forward. You can also choose a new series to connect over together. If you see cover art that makes your parental spidey-senses tingle, ask the store's attendant for more information or, better yet, your little comic book fan. Let them tell you why the art is not as scary as it looks and base your opinion on the maturity of their answer. If the response is, "Ha ha, blood is gross so it's cool," it might be too soon to break into a violent and complex comic series like *The Punisher*.

Maybe comic books are not how you want to engage with superheroes. Superheroes no longer only exist in the comic book world. Disney+ has the majority of the Marvel movie collection available to watch. Netflix and Hulu each host original series featuring superheroes from Marvel and DC. There is almost always a superhero movie playing at your local theater. Most children's TV channels also feature superhero shows like *Teen Titans GO!*, *Miraculous: Tales of Ladybug and Cat Noir*, and *Danger Force*. We can explore the effects of superhero mythology on our children even if we are not yet ready to dive into the world of comic books.

Whether your kid is into comic series or movie marathons, you should talk to them about their favorite superheroes and why they find them interesting. Discussions like these promote critical thought and empathy in our kids. When we learn what the most important character traits are from their perspective, we can use that information for a little self-reflection, too. Does your child like Superman because they idolize his overachievement? Maybe they are feeling a little too much pressure at home. Do they love Aquaman because he gets to spend more time with fish than people? Maybe you should discuss how comfortable they are feeling in their social circles. We discover ourselves through the stories we consume: how we feel, what we like and dislike, who we hope to be. The same goes for our kids.

Comic book stories and superheroes show us how powerful fictional characters can be for people. Whether they build futuristic nanotech suits, fly through the air, turn invisible, or punch harder than the average man, superheroes' real powers lie in their deep, complex feelings about what it means to be a human. Their stories give us a sense of connection, like we are finally being seen. From Superman's effort to sell war bonds in the 1940s to three Spider-Mans from different universes sharing a tear-jerking group hug in 2021, superheroes and comic book characters show us we are not alone in this world. We have each other and we are going to be okay, and that is one of the best lessons we can pass down to our children.

CHAPTER 10

POP CULTURE

*"Life moves pretty fast. If you don't stop
and look around once in a while, you could miss it."*
— Ferris Bueller, Ferris Bueller's Day Off

Has this ever happened to you?

It is a Tuesday night, you have finished with dinner, and you have two hours to kill before bedtime. You open up Netflix and see a new show. *Huh, that looks kind of interesting*, you think, but you do not want to commit to a new series right now. You choose to continue one of your other shows instead.

The next day at work, everyone around you is buzzing about the new show. They want to talk about all the characters, the plot twists, and the possibilities for next season. The rest of the week, it seems more people are watching it every day. Before you know it, most of your conversations include, "Have you seen that new show on Netflix?" All of your social media feeds are flooded with reviews, memes, and obscure comments about it.

You finally decide to sit down and see what all the fuss is about, and the show seems okay. You are a little upset about how much of it was spoiled, but at least you can participate in the ongoing conversation now. However, when you go into work and ask your coworker, "Have you seen that new show on Netflix?" she replies, "Yeah, it was great! Did you see that new movie on Amazon Prime?"

And just like that, it feels impossible to catch up.

Television series, movies, video games, podcasts, meme templates, music, and dozens of other forms of popular culture constantly shift in and out of favor. Fashion trends change several times a year. Celebrities rise and fall in popularity with every interview. Even food choices, like kale smoothies and avocado toast, grow and shrink in the public's eye. The fluctuation of pop culture is part of what makes the concept difficult to define. In its most simple form, pop culture is a collection of intellectual and artistic ideals that represent spiritual, aesthetic, and/or moral sensibilities within its given community.[37] As communities' collective interests and morals change, so do the interests within their pop culture.

Pop culture encompasses a wide range of interests and activities that stretches across multiple subsets (think what we have already covered, Anime, Dungeons and Dragons, Video Games, etc.). No one can engage with every part of pop culture—there is not enough time in a day to consume it all. We pick and choose our pop culture interests based on how closely they seem to present an aspect of our spiritual, moral, social, intellectual, economic, or political codes. While our interests and our kids' interests might not align, both are part of pop culture as a whole.

Every item in pop culture has its own set of **cultural artifacts**, or markers from their unique mythology. The band KISS has their iconic open-mouthed, tongue-stretched expression. The book, *The Catcher in the Rye*, has a carousel horse and Holden's gratuitous potty mouth. *Grease* has black and pink leather jackets. Any phrase, item, or character immediately recognizable from a specific pop culture title can be considered a cultural artifact when viewed on its own.

Cultural artifacts, when removed from their original mythos, represent our participation as fans. As an example, the four houses

---

[37] Jenkins, Henry, Tara McPherson, and Jane Shattuc. Defining Popular Culture. Duke University Press, 2002.

of Hogwarts have taken to denote personality descriptions never defined in the *Harry Potter* book series. T-shirts with slogans like "Vote for Pedro" and "Schrute Farms Bed & Breakfast" invoke deeper meaning to fans of *Napoleon Dynamite* and *The Office* than the general population. Two big circles separated by a curved line forms a shape recognizable as Mickey Mouse's head no matter how obscure the design—that's why the Disney Parks are capable of creating so many "Hidden Mickey" hunts across their properties. The basic shape is so recognizable that it can blend into hundreds of patterns, textures, and designs. Geek interests with easily recognizable cultural artifacts make recognition and participation easier for fans.

We use cultural artifacts as foundations to build our personal identity on. Our wardrobe, home decor, and accessories are often dictated by our pop culture interests. Many of us own band t-shirts from our favorite musicians or festivals. We decorate our computers, car bumpers, and refrigerators with images from our favorite shows. People with tattoos often have a few pieces representing fictional characters or stories that resonate with them in some way. The artifacts and interests we choose to display around us blend together to form our personal aesthetics, or tastes.

EXPRESS YOURSELF

Once you start looking for the ways people express themselves with pop culture artifacts, you will see examples everywhere. If you actively engage in pop culture expression, you've likely come across some variation of Funko's Pop! Dolls. These small figures all have similar features: big eyes, square heads, and tiny bodies. The dolls' basic design is decorated with a few defining features of characters from pop culture titles. The Chewbacca Pop! doll is brown with a studded belt across its chest. Ariel's doll has long red hair and a mermaid tail. Lebron James' figure has a beard and a Lakers jersey with a basketball tucked under its arm. Pop! dolls are an excellent example of the cheap, simple ways we express our pop culture interests in our cubicles, bedrooms, and other spaces we feel like decorating with our personality.

Displaying cultural artifacts allows us to relate to each other through our shared interests and experiences. At the 2020 Olympics, many athletes from around the world displayed cultural markers on their performance outfits. México's synchronized swimming pair wore suits with the Moon Spirit koi fish from *Avatar: The Last Airbender*. Several athletes struck signature poses from *One Piece* after completing their events. A Belgian gymnast revealed her good luck charm, a small statue of Link from *The Legend of Zelda* after winning a gold medal. Fans around the world cheered when they recognized references to one of their pop culture interests on an international stage. The athletes' pop culture references made audiences feel connected with them in a unique way.

Many pop culture fans name pets after favorite characters from pop culture titles. One of the most common dog names over the last decade is Milo, a nod to the 1986 film *The Adventures of Milo and Otis*. Even if the dog is a plucky Golden Retriever instead of a pug, people still appreciate the homage to a film they remember fondly. Similarly, one of the most common cat names is Oliver, after the 1988 classic, *Oliver and Company*. When we take our pets for a walk in the park and call after them, we signal our interests to anyone in earshot. This is a subtle, but intentional way we cast a wide net for finding other people who share our interests and beliefs.

For example, if a chocolate lab bounds up to me in the park and his owners run after him, hollering for Haku to stop jumping, I can guess with strong certainty the dog is named after a character from Studio Ghibli's classic movie, *Spirited Away*. Anyone can then choose to start a conversation with his owners based on that information. (Whether the motive is to make new friends or stall their departure to pet their dog a little more is to be determined.)

Not everyone will recognize each cultural artifact from pop culture; part of what makes pop culture so interesting is its expansiveness. Pop culture is a buffet of content and experiences. We choose the worlds and archetypes most meaningful to us and use them as a mode of expression to others. This curated form of self-expression allows for a myriad of potential relationships across multiple mediums. Ultimately, how we engage with pop culture directly affects how we relate to others.

I use *Pokémon* to relate to my son, but when my daughter reaches video gaming age, she may prefer community builders like *Animal Crossing* and *Stardew Valley*. My wife would rather enjoy a Netflix series together than play a video game, so I relate to her differently than I do my children. I relate to each of my clients through a different pop culture medium dependent on their interests. Pop culture is expansive enough to account for a wide variety of interests when forming relationships with other people in our lives.

Fandoms form around pop culture titles, and these communities relate to one another through their interests. Some fandoms have entire theme parks designed to indulge every facet of their interests. Disney World and Disneyland allow fans of Walt Disney Studios' classic characters and stories to explore a deeply immersive, fantasy experience. Universal Studios also uses pop culture artifacts to act as inspiration for thrill rides, live performances, and themed dining experiences. Legoland is another example of a theme park designed with its biggest fans' enjoyment in mind. In theme parks, communities are free to express their passion for fairytales, superheroes, and imaginative construction in an expansive recreational space full of fellow fans.

When fandoms are not vacationing in Florida or California, social media sites like Reddit and Tumblr host dedicated spaces for fandoms to interact. Internet discussion promotes cultural exchange, which influences and expands pop culture content for all parties. Almost every facet of pop culture has a dedicated subreddit for communities to discuss their interests. Tumblr has pages dedicated to fan art, fan made memes, and fan fiction stories for pop culture titles. Twitter communities often comment back and forth with each other in long threads of tweets. Social media allows fans across the world to discuss their favorite topics in pop culture. At a certain point, though, the access to thousands of theme parks' worth of pop culture in our home can become overwhelming...especially when our kids start engaging.

Our children can experience unique, engaging, and relatable conversation when they participate in communities or fandoms surrounding their favorite pop culture mythologies. This is important because it reassures kids that they are not alone in their interests, no matter how niche they may be. While our children should be monitored when using social media sites—not all easily accessible content is appropriate—their interaction with these online fandoms can provide parents with valuable insight into their kids' interests and beliefs. By observing the online communities our kids are engaging with, we can seek to understand our children's potential passions by examining how fans with similar interests interact amongst each other and express themselves. Then we can use our understanding of Geek Culture to help guide our kids' engagement. At a certain point, though, communities will find ways to evolve their favorite pop culture artifacts into their own forms of communication.

Cultural artifacts can be recontextualized from their original mythos to have different meanings for their fandoms. The Vulcan salute from Star Trek is understood as a greeting between

Star Trek fans, even though in the show it exists solely for Vulcan use. When *The Mandalorian* first aired on Disney+, "Baby Yoda" memes flooded the internet with pictures of Grogu saying cutesy phrases like, "chickie nuggies" and "choccy milk." In the show, Grogu is a perfectly capable being who is hundreds of years old. He saves the main character's life on several occasions. Still, because he is admittedly adorable, fans recontextualized his image to represent the audience's childlike tendencies. Cultural artifacts like Grogu's appearance allow us to put our own spin on our favorite pop culture titles to form a personal connection within its fan base.

Pop culture titles become popular because of their relatability to some aspect of the human experience. We consume pop culture to find ways to relate to the world around us. We look for examples of stories that inspire us, people we should avoid idolizing, and teams to root for while they complete their fictional journey. When a story becomes recognizable enough to be considered part of pop culture, we can use its presence to relate to a wider variety of people in our daily lives. Part of the human condition is an ongoing effort to make sense of our experience, and shared language from pop culture helps us organize our lives.

WHICH CHARACTER ARE YOU?

Personality quizzes, like The Sorting Hat Quiz from *Harry Potter* fandom, organize us into categories recognizable across multiple genres and styles to relate to one another. Even if we have not read *Harry Potter* or watched the movies, we most likely know the difference between a Slytherin and a Gryffindor. By identifying with a character or group from pop culture, we express how we perceive and interact with the world through a unique language built from cultural artifacts.

Society has been using pop culture organization for centuries. Popular medicine theory, developed by Hippocrates in Ancient Greece, gave us the Four Temperaments, which led practitioners to believe common behavior deviations were due to an imbalance of four bodily humors: blood, yellow bile, black bile, and phlegm. Phlegm represents our steadfastness and hesitancies, black bile represents our cautiousness and obsessiveness, yellow bile represents our dominance and depression, and blood represents our social influence and usefulness to society. Any trait lacking in a usually well-balanced person was considered to be a result of a shortage of its respective bodily fluid. While we now understand medical diagnoses as much more complex, the Four Temperaments theory was the first stepping stone in early personality tests used in psychology and pop culture.

We see the Four Temperaments, or Humors, test in pop culture today through fictional communities and characters. Traits commonly associated with each humor in Ancient Greece are still common in modern personality types, and content creators recognize their similarities and apply them to original characters. Take a look at this table to see how the four humors have evolved and found their place in some of the most iconic pop culture titles today.

Four Humors	Avatar: The Last Airbender	Disney Princesses	Friends
Blood (sanguine)	Air	Rapunzel	Phoebe & Joey
Phlegm (phlegmatic)	Water	Aurora	Chandler & Rachel
Black Bile (melancholic)	Earth	Queen Elsa	Ross
Yellow Bile (choleric)	Fire	Tiana	Monica

While there is still very little science providing merit to any personality test, we humans are, at the very least, intrigued to discover other people who fit into the same categories as we do. Having a common language to communicate deeper complexities of our personality is a powerful social lubricant. We use personality tests evolved from the Four Humors to better understand people as we form relationships with them, even though those people's personalities are similarly subject to evolution.

We can use personality tests to compare and contrast across multiple pop culture titles. A person might argue that because waterbenders also use bloodbending in *Avatar: The Last Airbender*, waterbending should be considered more aligned with sanguine. This could open up a discussion about literal and figurative interpretations of each humor and personality type, allowing us to relate personality types through a pop culture lens.

We might meet new friends who do not know which Disney princess would fit them best, but they know whether they are a

Chandler or a Monica from years of watching *Friends* reruns. When we have a shared interest within pop culture, we can relate the information we gather from personality tests to each other, and develop a stronger bond.

We can also use personality tests to measure our growth. Our favorite pop culture icons most likely fit into one of the categories listed above, and when we compare what about them resonates with us, we can see how they influence our personal growth. We may have started out as a melancholic, Earthy personality type, but as we have learned and grown, we settled into a more phlegmatic, Water-type. Maybe circumstances were tough the first time we checked our personality type, and the turbulence has since subsided. Maybe now we are feeling a loss of control in our lives, but when we take the test again, we might align with the choleric, Fire personality type. Framing our internal emotions, morals, and aesthetics through pop culture personality tests help us make sense of how we feel inside by relating complex traits to common character archetypes. This makes personality tests a powerful tool for communicating past friction with our loved ones.

Taking a personality quiz with your child can help you understand their wants and needs through common character tropes. If your results say you fall into the Fire category and your child is an Air-type, it may explain friction between the two of you as diametrically opposed personalities. You can use your personality tests' information to make special accommodations to improve the relationship between you and your child. While you might be more reserved and thoughtful, your child might fall into a category known for fun-seeking and spontaneity. They are more likely to be an extrovert, while you probably end up burning out quicker the more people you are around. Accommodations and compromises for each personality type can help you and your child experience the world together without exhausting one another.

Relating to characters in pop culture through similar personality archetypes is an intentional feature of the content. Creators use variations of the Four Temperaments formula to create relatable characters for their audience. TV shows, movies, novels, and other narrative forms of storytelling achieve success when their audience can relate to the characters' personalities and motivations. By following consistent formats to develop new characters, creators give the audience a piece of themselves to root for while they explore a fictional landscape. The creators receive positive reviews for building an engaging world and we, the audience, receive a new framework through which we can explore ourselves. The mediums through which we connect with pop culture are not limited to personality types; there are more options to explore.

MUSIC IN POP CULTURE

Pop culture is made up of more than character-based, narrative content; there are other forms of pop culture we can use to relate to our children. Music is an excellent form of self-expression most people relate to in pop culture. The evolution of music through streaming services like Spotify, Bandcamp, Soundcloud, and Apple Music make creating and consuming music easier than ever. New genres are constantly emerging, and their influence on pop culture is immense.

While classic rock was a large part of pop culture for a generation during a turbulent time in history, children and young adults today consider Electronic Dance Music (EDM) and Lo Fi music more relatable. EDM is an exciting, energetic genre meant to make its listeners engage with wild dance moves. And for music a bit more relaxing, it is not uncommon for our kids to have a playlist full of Lo Fi songs, which they play in the background while they read and study.

Communities and fandoms have always formed around music genres. Emo music is in the midst of a renaissance right now as bands from the early 2000s like My Chemical Romance, Paramore, and Nine Inch Nails experience a resurgence in concert events and album sales. Korean Pop, or K-Pop, is another genre emerging in pop culture with a dedicated fan base. While most listeners in the US do not understand the songs—most are sung in Korean—people still find the beats, melodies, and singers charming and entertaining enough to enjoy. Music provides a form of catharsis for its listeners, and fans with common emotional experiences can use their favorite music to share their experiences with others in their community.

Concerts, music festivals, and album releases all attract music fans to engage with each other. Some of the friendliest conversations between strangers happen in the outer halls of concert venues. Many groups of people who meet at music festivals keep in touch to attend more festivals together in the future. Album release dates are often posted by record companies in advance to generate conversation and excitement among fans. Music is emotionally powerful, and shared emotional experience is an excellent way to bond with others.

If we cannot drive our kiddos to a concert, or if we are not comfortable taking them to see an R-rated movie, we can find other ways to use pop culture to engage our family. As we discussed earlier, pop culture is massive. If we as parents attempt to keep up with every corner of the pop culture world, it will consume every waking moment of our day. Not only is the concept expansive, it also oscillates at head-spinning rates. Some of the most popular TV shows, songs, and movies today will slide off the pop culture slate into the realm of irrelevance tomorrow.

That is not always a bad thing, either—remember Gangnam Style? The ever-changing landscape also provides the benefit of some cultural items slipping into obscurity instead of sticking around as an earworm.

ENGAGING IN POP CULTURE

I remember the first time my mom used the word "cool" in front of me and my friends. We were browsing in a Toys-R-Us, and she found an electronic toy on a nearby shelf. She held it out to me and said, "Oh, look! This is really cool!"

My friends spun around to look at her. "What did you say?" one of them asked.

"I said this toy is really cool," she replied, turning the toy in her hands.

I squinted at her. "You've never used that word before."

"Yes I have," she said, "I use it all the time!"

I shook my head, "No you don't. Don't do that."

It shocked me to hear my mom so up-to-date on the slang I used with my friends. Every time new lingo emerged, like "wicked" or "radical," my mom was on top of it. She missed the mark when they faded out of use, though, and I teased her a few times. Now, as a parent, I understand how difficult it is to keep up with what is mainstream and what is considered irrelevant. By the time most parents start using lingo they have discovered to be popular with kids today, they are already two steps behind. This can become discouraging, but there are some tactics parents can use to help stay on top of pop culture evolutions as they occur.

One of the best ways to start engaging with your child's pop culture interests is to simply make yourself present while they engage on their own. When they hang out with their friends, pay attention to the pop culture references they make together. Make note of the movies, shows, and music they discuss. We can do this without eavesdropping by inviting our kids and their friends to spend time with us while we work around the house. If we are making dinner, we can ask them to help us chop veggies while they chat. While we clean the house, we can ask our kids to pick a music playlist while we tidy up. When they come home from a movie, we can ask for a synopsis. By participating in their pop culture interests, we encourage the idea that their opinions are important to us, and we begin to absorb the subtle shifts in pop culture as they take place.

When we participate in conversations with our kids and their friends, we want to avoid being a "helicopter" or "snowplow" parent. We do not want to interject our own thoughts and opinions about their interests. Interruptions like "back in my day…" and "it was better back when…" are dismissive and make our kids feel like their experiences are somehow less valuable than the ones you had growing up. Every generation experiences different facets of pop culture, even when certain aspects make resurgences. Before we feel like we have a solid understanding of how our kids experience pop culture, it is best for us to stay quiet while we absorb their interests and opinions.

That is not to say we cannot share aspects of our own pop culture with our kids. We can participate in ways that are not dismissive. We can *add* to their experience instead of *subtract* value from what they already enjoy. For example, if your kids and their friends are talking about a new game in class, ask if they want to learn how to make a Cootie Catcher or a paper football. Show them how you used to bond with your classmates and play a few rounds together. This way, we give them space to enjoy the pop culture surrounding them while also incorporating some of our own, creating a bond over a shared interest.

Some of the most popular titles from around the time we grew up are making a comeback today, which opens a new avenue for discussion with our kids. The *Star Wars* franchise, which was so influential when it first appeared in pop culture, is expanding its universe constantly. The *Teenage Mutant Ninja Turtles* are making their way back into the spotlight on kids' television networks. *My Little Pony* has long-running shows with a dedicated community. If you recognize a version of an interest you enjoyed as a child, engage in a discussion about the evolution of the characters with your child after watching it together.

Pokémon has been around since 1996. There have been over one thousand episodes of *Pokémon*, twenty-two films, and 122 video games as of the fall of 2021. Twenty-five years of Pokémon stories give my son and I a wide collection of content to relate through. While I began my *Pokémon* journey on a handheld console, my son and I engage in our shared pop culture interest through the augmented reality of *Pokémon Go*. As we walk through local parks and explore our community together, we take advantage of the opportunity to bond over something we both resonate with and enjoy.

There are many ways to explore pop culture with your child. When you are in the car together, ask them to plug in their listening device—whether it is a phone, iPod, or MP3 player—and play you some of their favorite music. It might not be the type of music you usually listen to, but even if you do not enjoy it in your free time, it gives you insight into how they are feeling right now. Is the music soft and sad or lively and loud? If the song is about chasing after a pretty girl, maybe they are in need of some romantic encouragement. Maybe the lyrics do not matter at all and your child is more intrigued by the bass or the guitar riffs underneath. Ask them what they like about their favorite songs and bands. Compare it to your favorite parts of *your* music and maybe, if they are feeling open to it, show them what is interesting about your own collection.

A fun exercise in self-expression is to decorate your own Funko Pop! dolls together, especially if you or your child already own a few. Funko has an option on their website to design your own Pop! avatar. They also sell DIY Pop! dolls as blank canvases. Pick two up from your local game shop, craft store, or online shopping sites and decorate them together. Paint your favorite outfits on your dolls and ask your child what they like about their chosen look. Ask what their distinguishing features would be and make them together out of modeling clay. Would their character hold a paintbrush? A book? Maybe your child comes up with a prop for their doll based on an interest you did not know about before. When your figures are complete, you have two tangible representations of your personalities to display and reflect on as your child grows up.

Enjoying pop culture titles with our kids also allows us to see how we as a society have shifted our values and priorities since we were growing up. While jocks and cheerleaders used to be the "cool" kids in school, as shown by iconic pop culture films like *The Breakfast Club, Fast Times at Ridgemont High*, and *Grease*, main characters in today's pop culture are more eclectic than ever before. The *Hunger Games* and *Divergent* series feature intelligent and capable main characters who were introverted outsiders in their communities before their journeys began. New takes on old classics like *Saved by the Bell, Boy Meets World*, and *That's So Raven* have appeared on network television with notable changes, including progressive attitudes, more diverse casts, and emphasis on geek culture's renaissance.

It is more important now than ever for parents to understand geek culture, because most geek culture outlets are arriving in the pop culture sphere. While anime was considered too dorky or geeky of a genre to participate in when it first reached North America, it is now a genre firmly set in pop culture. Anime shows appear on major streaming services, anime merchandise sells in big box stores, and there are dozens of podcasts dedicated to anime discussion.

The same phenomenon is occurring with superheroes and comic book stories—while it was difficult to find someone who could recite the Infinity Stones ten years ago, most people today can name at least one of the five off the top of their head. Even if they have not seen *The Avengers: Infinity War*, they have probably seen trailers, reviews, or memes from the movie. In fact, every geek culture facet we have covered so far in this book is experiencing its own renaissance.

When the population at large recognizes a part of geek culture, even if they only engage at a surface level, then the interest has ascended to pop culture status. For example, Archie Comics' characters from 1941 gained new fame in cultural conversation when they appeared in the 2017 teen drama series, *Riverdale*. The show quickly became one of the most popular series on Netflix. *Riverdale* put a darker spin on the classically light comic stories, and it also modernized most of the characters' adventures to keep the attention of modern teens. The show even follows a classic *Dungeons & Dragons* storyline throughout season 3 (though the game is called Gryphons & Gargoyles in the show). *Riverdale* brought some of the most coveted geek culture interests into the public eye, and more are gaining popularity every year.

So, now that we have begun to understand the importance of geek culture, we can see how its benefits are worthy of pop culture's attention. However, we still have a lot to learn about our kids and their pop culture interests. We want to find relatable topics of conversation, but we are not always going to get it right the first time. We might sound a little silly when we try to relate to our children by asking to "yeet the salt" at dinner. We might refer to their favorite show as "Trouble Force" instead of *Danger Force*, and our kids might make fun of us a little bit. That is okay. A Hero's job (and parents too!) is to make mistakes to show that failing forward is perfectly fine and that we can use it to our benefit.

As parents, we often assume we are supposed to be all-knowing, all-seeing figures in our childrens' lives. We assume we should never make mistakes or admit we are not keeping tabs on every new band, show, and celebrity in the spotlight at any given moment. We cannot reveal we have no idea who Ninja is or why Ellen DeGeneres was canceled. We do not even know what "sus" means, and at this point, we are too afraid to ask. When we subscribe to such demanding expectations from ourselves, we set ourselves up to fail. Like Captain Marvel realizes after she is knocked down for the umpteenth time, we must recognize we are only human. There is nothing wrong with failing in front of your kids. They fail in front of us, and we do not fault them for their momentary vulnerability.

We get knocked down, but we get up again. We use adversity and resilience to continue moving ourselves forward and keep sharing knowledge with our children that is crucial to their own development. When they see us model problem solving, they know they can do it as well.

We must attempt to separate ourselves from those limiting fears and beliefs. As for what you *should* subscribe to... Well, it is time we talk about the multi-billion dollar elephant in the room: the world of online streaming and esports.

CHAPTER 11

ESPORTS & STREAMING

"People want to see life somewhere else taking place. It's comforting. Don't you think?"
— David Letterman, 1998

Some of the most influential moments in American history were captured live on television. We laughed at Ashlee Simpson's lip-sync malfunction on *Saturday Night Live*. We collectively grieved the collapse of the Twin Towers. We tune in religiously for live coverage of Super Bowls, political debates, and the Olympics. When live TV captures momentous cultural shifts, we feel a special kind of importance knowing we witnessed a groundbreaking event as it happened.

The suspense of a live broadcast makes it interesting for viewers. We watch live coverage of sports games because we do not know which team is going to win, and neither does anyone else until one team beats out the other. Watching a Major League Baseball (MLB) or National Football League (NFL) game the day after it happened does not hold the same mystique as it did in real time. *Saturday Night Live* reruns are not as good on Sunday after the best blunders were edited out. Few people rewatch the Grammys because the suspense before the winner is announced does not feel the same during a rebroadcast. The feeling that "anything could happen" dissipates when the content is not live.

Live videos are still an influential part of our culture, but nowadays, most are available on the Internet instead of network broadcasting. Streaming content to viewers on laptops, tablets, and smartphones in real time has transformed the way we communicate. Rather than push highlight reels and content from "yesterday," social media feeds now prioritize live content first and foremost. People are more likely to engage in content that is relevant *at the moment*, and with new accessibility of streaming technology, there is no shortage of live digital content. At all hours of the day, streamers are broadcasting their best and worst moments for millions of people to tune in and watch.

The most common types of live videos on the Internet today are gaming videos. In a competitive setting, players participate in live gaming on livestreams. Every day, millions of people log into social media accounts like Twitch and YouTube to watch other people play video games. While watching other people play video games instead of playing the actual game might sound mundane, gaming livestreams have proven to be highly viewed events, even as popular as traditional sports themselves. When gamers compete in officially organized settings, they have entered the world of esports.

Esports and livestreaming share a few similarities. Electronic sports, or **esports**, are defined as a form of competition using video games, often in the form of organized, multiplayer competitions between players or teams. Livestreaming, or **streaming**, consists of broadcasting audio and/or video while simultaneously uploading the broadcast to the Internet. Esports are often streamed for spectators whether the competitions are in an arena or entirely virtual.

When COVID-19 regulations closed stadiums around the world, esports made their way into popular culture to fill the hole traditional sports left behind. Esports had already existed in the geek space well before the pandemic, but with live sports shut down, esports filled the entertainment gap for wider audiences, even airing primetime on ESPN. Tournaments still took place and prize money still baffled spectators, but there were some problems with the transition. Not all esports events were aired on popularly accessed sites. If people wanted to watch an esports tournament, they most likely needed to know about specific streaming sites, like Twitch.

Aside from professional esports, streaming on social media sites saw its own rise in popularity during the COVID-19 pandemic, but for different reasons. In mandated social isolation, millions of people suddenly found themselves bored and lonely. To keep in good health, we had to self-isolate, but humans are social creatures, and nature compels us to connect. Streaming provided a compromise where people could chat, laugh, and play games together through their computers or phones. It was free, easy, and quickly became a popular pastime.

Even as social distancing mandates eased, both the esports and livestreaming industries continued to flourish. Many who joined recreational esports leagues to pass time in lockdown were recruited to professional teams. Streamers looking to play a few rounds of *Among Us* with their buddies grew their viewership to the hundreds of thousands. In the wake of the pandemic, esports and livestreaming are quickly becoming two powerhouse industries in the online realm.

If they have access to the Internet, it is likely your child has watched a few streamers or esports players. They might have their favorite streamers or Twitch channels they like to watch every week, or even every day. Some parents worry that watching videos online all day will rot their kids' brains, or stop them from talking to real-world people. These concerns are valid, but the skills our kids can acquire from livestreams and esports are also valuable.

Our children have a unique opportunity when it comes to their relationships and future careers. The esports and livestream industries are still emerging. Engaging our children with esports and streaming might prompt them to explore a new talent, or maybe a new career path. However, both esports players and streamers face their own unique set of obstacles. If our children want to pursue either, we must help them succeed as little internet explorers.

ESPORTS

Esports competitions have been around for about as long as video games themselves. They began in bar tournaments for cabinet games like Pacman, Galaxia, and Centipede. The first winner of a worldwide Tetris competition took home the gold in 1990. Street Fighter made its way from dusty consoles in arcade corners to the Capcom Pro Tour 2021. Video games have always inspired competition, and esports developed as an industry to accommodate.

Today, many parents and non-gamers hear the term "esports" and immediately think it only applies to classic sports video games. Some parents recognize virtual sports games like *2K* for basketball, *FIFA* for soccer, and *Madden* for football. The Wii fans might remember playing baseball, tennis, and bowling with motion-capture controllers. However, the realm of esports stretches far beyond simulated versions of our limitations in the real world.

There are three main categories for modern esports competitions in the professional arena. First-person shooter games (FPSs) like *Counterstrike*, *Fortnite*, and *Valorant* consist of players on a team battling with others. Multiplayer Online Battle Arena games (MOBAs) like *League of Legends* are capture-the-flag, raid style games with large teams working together toward a common goal. Real Time Strategy games (RTSs) like *Starcraft 2* involve the players constructing the world around them outside of a turn-based order to overwhelm or destroy the enemy's base. Although these three categories are the most common in esports today, the industry stretches to almost all corners of the video game world.

As video games became more complex, so did the competitions. Esports tournaments now fill stadiums with 10,000 or more seats, hold opening ceremonies with complex performances, and *insane* pools of prize money to the victors. Esports competitions are as much of a spectacle as any professional sports game. However, while esports can be a fun alternative to traditional sports, they can be as physically and mentally demanding as their more physical counterparts.

Esports competitions are not too far off from traditional sports. Despite the players sitting in a chair all day, their work is demanding. Players are expected to dedicate the majority of their day to practicing for upcoming competitions. Some training schedules last ten to sixteen hours a day. Esports players are held to professional standards and are required to devote their lives to the competition as long as they are playing.

If your children are interested in esports, they may set themselves up for a career path as lucrative and demanding as any professional sports player. Not unlike the NFL or NBA, esports players are often recruited from high school or college and offered hefty salaries. The average annual income of an esports professional is around $410,000. Players can earn tournament money on top of their base income, too. The International 2021 tournament, awarded $40 million to be split among the winning teams. In addition to a hefty paycheck, your child can earn lifelong skills from the esports industry.

Esports players can gather valuable lessons similar to the ones earned in traditional sports. Most professional esports players are part of a team. They socialize with their teammates. They collaborate with others to accomplish a common goal. They learn to see themselves as a valuable, contributing member of a group. Some esports leagues provide housing for their players, called "gaming houses" to live and practice together to promote an even stronger team bond.

Gaming houses expose players to different cultures and languages. Esports compete at an international level, which means recruiters for major esports leagues sometimes recruit from other countries to stack their teams. Not all players from other countries are able or willing to find housing for themselves, so the leagues help them settle and integrate into the team's culture in gaming houses. It is not uncommon for a gaming house to have players from China, Korea, Japan, Norway, and the USA all living under one roof.

Multicultural exposure is invaluable for developing teenagers. Living together under one roof, eating together, and practicing together for upcoming competitions is meant to inspire a sense of camaraderie and teamwork between players. However, it also makes it difficult to overcome language barriers to communicate about who's turn it is to do the dishes and who left a wet towel on the bathroom floor.

Working, living, and breathing esports as a career can be exciting for some players, but such a competitive and demanding environment is not without its health risks. As with any athletic sport, players can burn out easily. Esports players hit their stress maximums like anyone else would after working nonstop for more than eight hours a day.

Whether your child is interested in becoming a world-renowned esports player or a recreational player who occasionally competes in local tournaments, there are some special health considerations parents should remain aware of to keep their children happy and healthy.

PRESSING PAUSE

Some people hear about professional video game players and think, *"They're being paid to play games, that's the easiest job in the world!"* It sounds like a fun gig, but many fail to consider how esports players face similar stressors in their job as other professionals. When a game becomes the source of income, identity, and intrinsic value, it stops being a game and starts being a dependency.

"I just thought I'd get to play video games for a living," said professional League of Legends player Jason Tran, "I didn't really know how much effort and time you actually have to put in to compete at the highest level. The general public thinks that pro players are just having fun, making money and playing video games and it's all very easy, but I don't think that's the case at all."

Jason "WildTurtle" Tran has been playing esports professionally since 2012. His current team, FlyQuest, recently launched a sustainability initiative to bring attention to the mental health struggles many esports players face today. Most professional esports players limit their careers to five to ten years before they retire. Esports players require superhuman reflexes and reaction times. Professionals practice for ten to sixteen hours a day, which takes a toll on their wrists, backs, and necks. Players between the ages of eighteen and twenty-four are typically considered in their esports "prime," and most retire around the age of twenty-five. Some retired players move into a coaching role. Some are so burnt out from their time in the industry they switch career paths altogether.

Since professional gamers are not perceived to experience stress comparable to other professional athletes, they are often left struggling physically and mentally without support. Some professional gamers have resigned in the middle of a season, citing mental health concerns. Some players ended up in the hospital for stress-related injuries. As parents, it is our responsibility to recognize signs of mental and physical health decline in our kids and mitigate them as soon as possible.

There are several ways to ensure our kids are competing in healthy ways. The first and most important way to improve healthy play time is to schedule intermittent breaks from gaming. Kids need moments to press pause and shake off pent up gaming frustration, desk chair cramps, and those little wigglies in the corner of their vision. They may not be so willing to take these breaks at first, but once they experience how the breaks benefit them, they may be more willing to put down the controller.

We know video games do not cause aggression to appear out of thin air in players, but we also know spending too much time doing *anything* can reduce our frustration tolerance. Whether you are trying to thread a needle, plug in a USB, or beat a difficult level in *Ratchet & Clank*, we lose our patience when seemingly simple tasks are barely out of reach. As the day goes on, esports players' patience dwindles, and since they are expected to practice for hours on end, their frustration tolerance deteriorates, too. It is unavoidable to play a game with the same readiness, focus, and frustration tolerance from hour one to hour nine. The players need breaks.

If players do not take breaks, they run the risk of internalizing their failures when their shortcomings are simply a result of overworking. Players might think they cannot beat the other team because they are not good enough, they were never good enough, and they were fooling themselves ever thinking they *would* be good enough. Negative self-talk like this can lead our kiddos down a dangerous path. We want to encourage them to stop, take a beat, and reset. Half an hour breaks every two hours make a world of difference in improving their mental health, frustration tolerance, and overall gaming performance. These breaks are also crucial for maintaining physical health.

Players have to give their eyes a break from endlessly scanning monitors for enemies and mission goals. Their backs need stretching and their legs need circulation. Their wrists must relax from their cramped positions above the mouse and keyboard. Humans are not meant to stay still for long periods of time, and the ten to sixteen hour workday of an esports player is not conducive to physical health. Taking screen breaks and moving around throughout the day will keep players in better shape.

The second best way to encourage a healthy relationship between your children and esports is to involve yourself. Be their biggest fan! Soccer moms and football dads sit in the stands for their kids' games, but with an esports player, you can cheer your child on from a more comfortable chair than aluminum bleachers. You can also cheer as loud as you want without receiving weird looks from quieter parents. Video games can be as fun to watch as they are to play, so try it out.

When your child sees you engaging with their play and encouraging them, they are more likely to feel validated. Kids want their parents' approval, even if they do not say it out loud. When we encourage them to use their skills and succeed at pursuing their interests, we inspire them to improve, persevere, and celebrate their victories.

If your child does not want to pursue a career as a professional esports player, it is perfectly okay. Not every parent with kids on a tee ball team is expecting the next Babe Ruth or Derek Jeter. There are other ways for your child to develop their esports passion. While professional esports players dedicate the majority of their time to practicing and competing, many players take an alternative route into the world of livestreaming.

LIVESTREAMING

The esports industry would not be nearly as popular as it is today without the introduction of streaming. Livestreamers broadcasting their competitions through Twitch, YouTube Live, and other platforms brought attention to esports' value as a spectator sport. This encouraged sponsors, broadcasters, and other stakeholders to invest in the streaming industry. Gaming and esports streams are the most popular live content online. Esports and streaming overlap with each other in many ways, but livestreaming has a unique set of concerns for parents.

Streaming gained popularity quickly because of its accessibility. Anyone with a microphone, camera, and internet connection has the ability to stream instantly. Early streamers got their start playing games, exploring local hangout spots, or simply spending time chatting with viewers from their bedroom. The interactive nature of streaming made both streamers and their audiences feel connected. Social media apps quickly pounced on the potential livestream market, and now most major social media apps feature a livestreaming component.

Livestreaming is exciting when the content and the creator are engaging. Livestreamers might range from your Aunt Betty who occasionally pops into Facebook Live to chat with anyone online, to full-blown celebrities going live at a scheduled time to interact with fans. Livestreaming allows simple, interactive connection with other people in real time. There is a certain spontaneity viewers and creators find captivating when they tune into a livestream. There is someone there on the other side of the screen, right now, watching the same content as you.

Streaming is one of the main ways our children's generation consumes content. On average, 22 percent of children ages four to sixteen are creating their own streaming content, and 41 percent are watching others' content on a regular basis.[38] Whether your children livestream videos or watch livestreams made by other people, they are participating in a relatively new form of online communication. It is normal for parents to have some concerns or fears about livestreaming. As long as we take necessary precautions with our children, we can allow them to take advantage of the benefits livestreaming has to offer.

Streaming can provide a method for people to engage in live events regardless of distance, budget, or other restrictions. Some creators livestream concerts and other events to their audience. If your child desperately wants to go see a live concert across the country, but you do not want to pay for travel or have your kids miss school, you can compromise by watching a livestream of the show together. Grandparents who cannot travel to see their grandkids in the school play can watch the whole show via livestream. Churches can livestream services to an online congregation to make sermons more accessible. Any event without recording restrictions can be livestreamed to make people at home feel included.

Livestreams also allow people to connect with others who share their interests. When one of your child's favorite streamers begins a livestream titled, "My Top Ten Favorite Pokémon," and two hundred viewers log in to watch, those two hundred people probably like Pokémon, too. They want to hear the streamer's opinion, debate in the comments section, and provide their own opinions for other viewers to comment on. The video opened a dialogue for hundreds of people across the planet to discuss a common interest on a single platform.

A popular subgenre of livestreams called "Reaction Videos" allows viewers to identify emotionally with others. Streamers play a song, movie, or TV show and explain their feelings about it out

---

[38] "Parents Guide to Live Streaming and Vlogging." Internet Matters. Accessed January 20, 2022. https://www.internetmatters.org/resources/parents-guide-to-live-streaming-and-vlogging/#parents_concerns_views.

loud for the audience. If a song is funny they might laugh out loud. If a show has a shocking moment they might gasp or scream. They might talk out a confusing moment and ask questions to the audience. These types of videos are especially popular because they allow viewers to compare their own reactions to the streamer's reaction and feel connected over similar emotional experiences.

Some livestreams of TV shows or movies allow groups to tune in and watch together, whether they live alone or do not have anyone at home who enjoys the same kind of television. Viewers can comment in real time with theories, opinions, and reactions to the show to immediately share them with the audience. Livestreams like these add a level of interaction to a hobby some people may find lonely.

Most celebrities or "influencers" who hold our kids' attention exist primarily on the Internet, whether through livestreaming or video blogs (vlogs). Our kids use these videos to stay up to date on trends and pop culture. They also collect tips about style, organization, and socialization from celebrities, content that used to only be available through magazines and newspaper write-ups. The urge to belong and connect is the same, but this generation fills it through the Internet instead of magazines thanks to innovations in technology.

Livestreaming can also provide emotional and financial support for creators. Similar to esports, streaming live content and cultivating a large enough following can be a lucrative business. Some streaming platforms offer the ability to earn revenue based on views. Sponsors sometimes reach out to streamers and pay them to promote products. Streamers can offer exclusive content—like shoutouts in game chats, early access to content, and even merchandise—to their followers in exchange for payment through subscription services like Patreon. Depending on the content, creators have a variety of avenues through which they can monetize their material.

For example, Critical Role, a streaming channel dedicated to *Dungeons & Dragons* campaigns, raked in $9.5 million in revenue in 2021 in Twitch viewership alone. Critical Role began streaming under their own name in 2018 and have since branched into podcasts, merchandise, animation, and more industries to maximize profits and influence.

If your child is interested in livestreaming, they should do it because they enjoy the experience, not because they are interested in making as much money as Critical Role. Some channels never receive more than a view or two on their videos. The purpose of the activity does not have to be money or a big audience. Maybe your child enjoys the act of recording, editing, and marketing their videos. Streamers can learn and experience exciting benefits regardless of follower count, but for big channels, the job can be demanding.

Live streaming requires strong multitasking skills. Streamers must remain "on" in front of the camera, interact with viewers in the chat, discourage or ban inappropriate discussion, promote even more interactions, and actually *do* whatever they are streaming. It is challenging to take it all on at once, even for an adult.

As their audience grows, streamers feel a sense of accomplishment and self-worth. Watching a viewer count rise on a stream feels similar to telling a story at a party and realizing the whole room has stopped to listen. You sparked interest in a group of people and now they want to hear what you have to say. It can be overwhelming, but it can also provide a space to be creative and engaging. You are the center of attention for a moment, which feels exhilarating.

When a streamer provides content like video game speedruns, makeup tutorials, or how-to drawing videos, they have the opportunity to gain confidence in their capabilities. Teaching another person how to do a task is one of the best ways to prove your expertise, and livestreaming adds a bit of pressure to the demonstration. Streamers post how-to videos on all kinds of topics: how to build a cardboard fort, how to paint a sunset, and best ways to wrap Christmas presents. When a streamer finishes with a beautiful fort or a crisp-cornered gift, they experience the product of their self-expression and they get to share it with their audience.

Streamers create easily accessible resources for pretty much any form of entertainment your children want to see. Want to know how to find the secret chest in *Breath of the Wild*? Want to learn how to perfect the "smokey eye" look? Want to know what Zendaya is up to today? There is more than likely a livestream happening right now to satisfy their curiosity.

However, with great accessibility comes great responsibility. Streaming is easy, so it creates the temptation to stream all the time in case someone is waiting to watch. We parents know not everyone on the Internet is friendly all the time. There are consequences to broadcasting life live online, and it is best to take an active role in our child's streaming experience to limit the mental health impact from livestreaming and viewing livestreams.

AND WE'RE LIVE IN 3...2...

Imagine yourself back at the dinner party where everyone in the room is tuned in to your story. You started telling it to two people, and now ten people are listening. You notice your larger audience, so you raise your voice, throw in a little more enthusiasm, and embellish a few details.

You must have gone too far, because two people turn around and leave the room. You dial it back and four people walk in to listen. You make a mental note to keep the pace, but now five people are leaving. You keep trying even though people are not engaging with you as much as before. You thought you saw a friend of yours here earlier, but she is not in the room anymore.

What are you doing wrong?

Livestreaming can feel like this. Watching viewers go in and out of your broadcast, and constantly adjusting your personality to provide the most "watchable" content for viewers takes a mental toll on you. Gaining viewers can be exciting, but losing viewers can feel like a personal failure. It is easy to internalize the feeling as a reflection of self-worth, especially if you've come to consider more regular viewers as friends.

Some streamers inflate the value of their viewers and followers. I have had clients burn themselves out in front of the camera and refuse to stop streaming because of their follower count. They were afraid to stop putting out content because it might shrink their list of followers and viewers. I have to tell them those people are not their friends, and if they were, they would understand taking time off to improve mental health. My clients' false concept of followers as friends was detrimental to their well-being, and I recommended they take a break.

When streamers broadcast for hours at a time, they are bound to catch a mistake or two. Accidents happen all the time. We might trip on the last step coming downstairs. We might dribble a little water down our shirt while taking a drink. We might stumble on a word or two while speaking. These missteps are in reality, quite minor, but imagine making any of these mistakes live, on camera. Suddenly, the small embarrassment from saying "muddle of pud" instead of "puddle of mud" is magnified hundreds, if not thousands of times over. Kids need breaks from livestreaming to come back to reality and remember whose opinions matter most to them.

Unpredictable moments occur all the time in the real world, and while some result in a shared laugh between streamers and viewers, some are not laughing matters at all. There is no thirty-second buffer like there used to be on live television. Inappropriate content can appear through racist, homophobic, sexist, or otherwise hateful comment before a moderator catches it. The same language might come from a person in the livestream, although it is rare, because creators must adhere to their platform guidelines to remain monetized. We want to supervise our kids' engagements with people online the same as we would if they were chatting on the street.

As parents, the best way to allow our children to view live content is to watch it with them. When we watch, we can monitor for appropriateness and answer any questions they might have about unexpected material. We can familiarize ourselves with their favorite internet personalities and assess the content. Until a Ratings Board exists for online content creators, there is no surefire way to predict the suitability of a channel for our children without watching it first.

For times when we cannot sit and watch livestreams with our kids, we can enact parental controls. Most platforms have controls to block content. Many also have "report" buttons for when content that previously passed parental controls becomes inappropriate. We can discuss with our children what kind of content is okay for them, not okay for them, and not okay *ever*. When we teach them to use report buttons, we allow them to strengthen their responsibility to the streaming community through participation. Even if our children are not interested in creating live content, their interactions with those who do should benefit the community.

If our children *do* become interested in livestreaming, the best way to monitor their content is to watch them create it. Livestreams cannot be edited, and once they are online, they can be tough to take down. It is a good idea to have a discussion with your child about what is allowed on camera and what is not. Some important guidelines to discuss with your child before turning on the camera might include:

- Personal information should not appear in a livestream. This includes discussing information like names, phone numbers, and addresses, but also information that might appear in the room around them, like street signs and the name of their school. It might be worth streaming from a public place instead of a bedroom or living room to ensure privacy.
- Peer pressure should not make them act differently to impress their viewers. Many livestreamers perform outrageous or dangerous stunts to grow their audience. We can livestream to entertain others, but not if it means acting in a way that makes anyone uncomfortable, or puts anyone in physical danger.
- No one should be included in a livestream without their consent. Remember to ask for permission before filming someone else. Everyone has a right to their own privacy, and if they do not want to be included in a video, they should not have to be in one.
- You never know who might see your content online— a future employer, a potential friend, or a bully. Remember to use good judgment when the camera is on and know when to put it away.

When we engage in esports and livestreaming with our children, we learn as much about them as they learn about the world. We see how they view competition through esports. We learn about their interests through their streaming habits. We can watch their personalities shine when they stream themselves. Even if they are only interested in one part of one industry, we can engage with them and form a strong bond around a common interest.

Live streamers, esports players, and other internet personalities are only going to rise in popularity as the industries continue to innovate and grow. Esports teams are already introducing Augmented Reality (AR) and Virtual Reality (VR) aspects into some of their competitions. Politicians have taken to streaming platforms to discuss issues directly with younger audiences. The covid pandemic encouraged people to seek out new ways to connect online since we could not connect in person, and livestreaming and esports proved to be valuable options for interaction.

New forms of online communication provide resources for learning new information, meeting new people, and gaining new experiences. There is a parental instinct to shield our kids from the Internet to protect them from dangerous content. We have to be careful, though, because if we block everything, we block educational opportunities, too. The esports and livestreaming industries appeal to our kids, so we will make more progress if we teach responsible internet usage and let them enjoy their content. And that is ultimately what superhero parenting is about: engaging with kids through the cultures they love to teach them responsibility, rather than taking away their passions from them.

CONCLUSION

"I have nothing left to say! You're the authority now!"
— Professor Oak

Every parent wants to be a superhero for their child, but no parent is born with superpowers. Like Iron Man, Black Widow, and Batman, we have to use what we have at our disposal to equip ourselves for the heroic journey of parenthood. Instead of super speed or X-Ray vision, we can use knowledge, patience, and strong communication skills to protect our children from harm. We might not succeed every day, but we continue to make an effort, and that is a heroic task in itself.

No hero's journey begins with a perfect character who has already mastered heroism. Thor, God of Thunder, began his story with a partying problem and a holier-than-thou attitude. Ash Ketchum begins his journey to become a Pokémon Master with an inferiority complex and an unearned sense of pride. Characters created for a D&D campaign begin at Level 1. Parenting is no different; we start with more questions than answers, and we fail our way forward until we reach success.

Failing is one of the most important things a human can do, because when we *fail*, we learn from our mistakes and increase our critical thinking skills. Persevering through repeated failure is a permeating lesson throughout geek mythology. Whether we are failing through a video game, watching our favorite TV characters fail their way to a season finale, or reading about comic book heroes learning from their shortcomings, we are learning how to fail gracefully.

Failing is just as important for parents as it is for kids. We are not going to make the right decision every time we parent our children. We are going to make choices out of anger, frustration, and sadness. We are going to make mistakes and get knocked down. As long as we get back up and put meaningful effort into being the heroic parent our children need, we are still moving forward.

When we inevitably make mistakes along our parenting journey, we have to ask ourselves where our misguided emotions are coming from. If we have restricted our kids from their geek interests in the past, we must reconcile our decisions with our internal motivations. Did we fear D&D's influence? Were we concerned that video games distracted our kids from their schoolwork? Did we ban anime because we found the voices too shrill? Once we understand the root of our choices, we can work on mitigating our concerns and instead start encouraging our children to explore their interests with healthy boundaries in place.

There is nothing wrong with failing as a parent as long as we use our failures to move forward. When we allow ourselves to learn from our misguided actions, we teach our children how to do the same. Every choice we make acts as a model for our children. When we act in both negative and positive ways toward our children, we must take a step back and recognize the role we want to play in their lives…before we act more like a villain than a hero.

Here is an example of failing forward through a shared interaction with me and my son getting dressed in the morning. My villainous side showed after my wife taught my son how to layer clothes. He came downstairs three mornings in a row with a beaming smile, springy step, and seven layers of shirts. Normally, I would have encouraged his dedication and enthusiasm to master a new skill, but his process resulted in both of us being late, so I found it less charming and more frustrating. On the third morning, I told him to change *again*, but my insistence confused him.

"But Mom said—"

"I know what Mom said," I cut him off, "but it's seventy degrees outside. You can't wear so many layers."

I dismissed his questions while I ushered him into the car. He stared down at his lap for the ride to school, quiet. After I dropped him at school and had the car to myself, I realized I had acted more as a villain than a heroic parent.

We must understand what villainy looks like when we are too aggressive with our children. Are our spikes out? Are we shooting fire out of our mouths? We must recognize when we are showing villainous tendencies—a raised voice, a sharp tone, a towering stance over our little ones—and how those actions are received.

When our children begin to avoid eye contact, portray closed-off body language, and avoid asking us questions or engaging with us, we know we have veered off the path of heroism and induced a shame response. Luckily, children are resilient, and mine shows the same progress as others while we continuously work on resiliency together.

Once I realized I acted as a villain with my son, I knew I would need to communicate with him so we could find a way to practice his new skill without delaying our morning routine. I needed to explain to him where my frustration came from, and I needed to apologize for directing it at him instead of expressing it to him. I wanted him to know even though I do not get it right every time, my goal is to guide him through the world and encourage his exploration.

These conversations, the ones in which we return to an event and address it, are key to any parenting ability. When we revisit conflict and unravel it with our children, we remove any remaining tension from the relationship, foster communication, and make room for both sides to explore their feelings.

Boundaries and ground rules are set by heroic and villainous parents alike, but the difference comes from the effort we put into helping our children understand the logic behind our limitations. Phrases like, "Because I said so," and, "My house, my rules," discredit our children's natural inclination to understand how the world works. Communication is a tool for heroes, and it is one of the most powerful tools we have at our disposal. We can use communication to engage with our children instead of imposing our rule over them.

Raising great children is a great responsibility. We must hold ourselves accountable to the role we have chosen to take on as parents. We can act as heroes for our children by setting aside time to engage them on their level. We can communicate with them in ways that invite their curiosities about the world. And when we make a mistake, we can communicate our shortcomings and try to do better next time. As our children's heroes, we are each setting an example for how they should navigate the world.

Our children learn as much from us as they do from their geek interests. We are constantly giving little pieces of ourselves to our kids, so we want to make sure the pieces we hand down are the best we have to offer. We cannot pass down superhuman strength or a magical family heirloom to our children before they start on their own hero's journey. Instead, we can teach them how to engage with the world openly, kindly, and patiently by engaging in their world with the same traits. By acting heroically, we build our children into heroes with the resiliency and perseverance to take on the world. And to this purpose, geek culture is an invaluable tool to help them slay any metaphorical dragons they will encounter on their personal journey.

Geek culture's mythologies help our children prepare for their personal journey. We now know how different aspects of geek culture encourage skills like critical thinking, empathy, communication, morality, perseverance, resilience, self-confidence, and dozens of others. Children who engage with geek culture are not only learning from one world, they are learning from thousands of worlds created specifically to encourage introspection and empathetic catharsis. When we explore geek culture with our children, we guide them through galaxies filled with stories, characters, and life lessons. We prepare them for the myriad of difficult choices they will make when they eventually set off on their own monomyth.

Until they hear The Call, we will be right there with them, prepared to take on the next adventure together. Like the wise Sage, spend no time fretting the small stuff. Focus on being the mentor your child wants and needs to help them get through their life. Hand off your heroism and give them the training they require to become a hero in their own right.

GLOSSARY

AI	Artificial Intelligence
AIM	American Online Instant Messenger
AMA	American Movie Association
AR	Augmented Reality
BFI	Big Five Inventory
CCA	Comics Code Authority
D&D	Dungeons & Dragons
DDR	Dance Dance Revolution
DM	Dungeon Master
EDH	Elder Highlander Commander
EDM	Electronic Dance Music
ESRB	Entertainment Software Rating Board
GM	Game Master
FPS	First Person Shooter
GTA	Grand Theft Auto
LARP	Live-Action Role Play
LFGS	Local Friendly Game Store
MCU	Marvel Cinematic Universe
MMO	Massively Multiplayer Online Game
MMORPG	Massively Multiplayer Online Role-Playing Game
NES	Nintendo Entertainment System
NPC	Non-Playable Character
PC	Personal Computer
PC	Playable Character
PvE	Person versus Environment
PvP	Person versus Person
PUBG	Player Unknown's Battleground
RP	Role-Play
RPG	Role-Playing Game
RTS	Real-Time Strategy
TCG	Trading Card Game
TTRPG	Tabletop Role-Playing Game
VR	Virtual Reality
WHO	World Health Organization

REFERENCES

Abyeta, S., & Forest, J. (1991). Relationship of Role-Playing Games to Self-Reported Criminal Behaviour. *Psychological Reports, 69*(3 suppl), 1187–1192. https://doi.org/10.2466/pr0.1991.69.3f.1187

Agronin, M. (2009). Group therapy in older adults. *Current Psychiatry Reports, 11*(1), 27-32.

American Psychiatric Association. (2013). *Diagnostic and statistical manual of mental disorders (DSM-5®)*. American Psychiatric Pub.

Andel, R., Hughes, T. F., & Crowe, M. (2005). Strategies to reduce the risk of cognitive decline and dementia. Aging Health, 1(1), 107-116.

Aoyama, Y., & Izushi, H. (2003). Hardware gimmick or cultural innovation? Technological, cultural, and social foundations of Japanese video game industry. *Research Policy, 32*(3), 423–444.

Apperley, T. H. (2006). Genre and game studies: Toward a critical approach to video game genres. *Simulation & Gaming, 37*(1), 6–23.

Argyle, M., & Henderson, M. (1985). The rules of relationships. In S. Duck & D. Perlman (Eds.), Understanding relationships: An interdisciplinary approach (pp. 63–84). Beverly Hills, CA: Sage

Ascherman, L. I. (1993). The Impact of Unstructured Games of Fantasy and Role Playing on an Inpatient Unit for Adolescents. *International Journal of Group Psychotherapy, 43*(3), 335–344. https://doi.org/10.1080/00207284.1993.11732597

Ayres, J., & Malouff, J. M. (2007). Problem-solving training to help workers increase positive affect, job satisfaction, and life satisfaction. European Journal of Work and Organizational Psychology, 16, 279-294.

Bandura, A. (1977). Social Learning Theory. New York: General Learning Press.

Bandura, A. (1986). Social Foundations of Thought and Action. Englewood Cliffs, NJ: Prentice-Hall.

Banks, J., Bowman, N. D., & Wasserman, J. A. (2017). A Bard in the Hand: The Role of Materiality in Player–Character Relationships. *Imagination, Cognition and Personality*, 0276236617748130. https://doi.org/10.1177/0276236617748130

Barnett, D. (2016, August 21). Hugo awards see off rightwing protests to celebrate diverse authors. *The Guardian*. Retrieved from https://www.theguardian.com/books/2016/aug/21/hugo-awards-winners-nk-jemisin-sad-rabid-puppies.

Barreto, M., & Ellemers, N. (2000). You can't always do what you want: Social identity and self-presentational determinants of the choice to work for a low status group. *Personality and Social Psychology Bulletin*, (26), 891–906.

Barsanti, S. (2018, January 15). Some creep made an overly sexist edit of *The Last Jedi* and even they think it's awful. *AVClub*. Retrieved from https://www.avclub.com/some-creep-made-an-overtly-sexist-edit-of-the-last-jedi-1822104868.

Bean, A. M. (2018). *Working with video games and game in therapy: A clinician's guide*. New York: Routledge.

Beauchamp, M. H., & Anderson, V. (2010). SOCIAL: An integrative framework for the development of social skills. Psychological Bulletin, 136(1), 39-64. doi:http://dx.doi.org.tcsedsystem.idm.oclc.org/10.1037/a0017768

Beck, J. S., & Beck, A. T. (2011). *Cognitive therapy: Basics and beyond* (2nd ed.). New York: Guilford press.

Bennett MP, Lengacher C. Humor and Laughter May Influence Health: III. Laughter and Health Outcomes. *Evidence-Based Complementary and Alternative Medicine*, March 2008.

Benson, J. (2001). Work at the ending stage of the group: separation issues. In Benson, J. (Ed), *Working more creatively in groups*, (145–54), Abingdon, England: Routledge.

Bessiere, K., Kiesler, S., Kraut, R., & Boneva, B. (2012). Longitudinal effects of internet uses on depressive affect: A social resources approach. In *American Sociological Association*. Philadelphia, PA.

Bird, J. M. & Markle, R. S. (2012). Subjective well-being in school environments: Promoting positive youth development through evidence-based assessment and intervention. American Journal of Orthopsychiatry, 82, (1), 61-66.

Blackmon, W. D. (1994). Dungeons and dragons: The use of a fantasy game in the psychotherapeutic treatment of a young adult. *American Journal of Psychotherapy*, *48*(4), 624–632.

Blinka, L., & Smahel, D. (2007). "Role-playing" games in the context of analytical psychology. *Ceskoslovenska Psychologie*, *51*(2), 169–182.

Boccamazzo, R., & Connell, M. (2019, November). The Applied Use of TTRPGs. *Gamehole Con*. Seminar conduced from the Aliant Energy Center Exhibition Hall, Madison, WI.

Bodrova, E., & Leong, D. J. (2015). Vygotskian and Post-Vygotskian Views of Children's Play. *American Journal of Play, 7*, 371-388.

Bogost, I. (2011). *How to do things with videogames*. U of Minnesota Press.

Bowman, S. L. (2010). *The functions of role-playing games: how participants create community, solve problems and explore identity*. Retrieved from http://public.eblib.com/choice/publicfullrecord.aspx?p=517013

Bowman, S. L. (2013). Social Conflict in Role-Playing Communities: An Exploratory Qualitative Study. *International Journal of Role-Playing*, (4), 4–25.

Bowman, S. L., Lieberoth, A. (2018). Psychology and role-playing games. In J. P. Zagal & S. Deterding (Eds.), *Role-Playing Game Studies* (pp. 245-264). New York: Routledge.

Brewer, M. B. (1991). The Social Self: On Being the Same and Different at the Same Time. *Personality and Social Psychology Bulletin*, *17*(5), 475–482.

Brickman, P., Coates, D., & Janoff-Bulman, R. (1978). Lottery winners and accident victims: Is happiness relative? Journal of Personality and Social Psychology, 37, 917–927.

Bryant, F. B. (2003). Savoring beliefs inventory (SBI): A scale for measuring beliefs about savoring. Journal of Mental Health, 12, 175–196.

Campbell, A., Converse, P. E., & Rodgers, W. (1976). The quality of American life. New York, NY: Russell Sage. Carver, C. S., L

Capcom. (2017). Capcom Annual Report. Retrieved April 18, 2019, from http://www.capcom.co.jp/ir/english/data/pdf/annual/2017/annual_2017_01.pdf

Caplan, S., Williams, D., & Yee, N. (2009). Problematic Internet use and psychosocial well-being among MMO players. *Computers in Human Behavior*, *25*(6), 1312–1319. https://doi.org/10.1016/j.chb.2009.06.006

Carle A. (2007). More than a game: brain training against dementia. *Nursing Homes: Long Term Care Management*, *56*(8), 22–61. Retrieved from http://search.ebscohost.com.tcsedsystem.idm.oclc.org/login.aspx?direct=true&db=ccm&AN=106167910&site=ehost-live

Carter, A. (2011). Using Dungeons and Dragons to Integrate Curricula in an Elementary Classroom. In M. Ma, A. Oikonomou, & L. Jain (Eds.) *Serious Games and Edutainment Applications* (pp. 329-246). New York, NY: Springer. DOI: 10.1007/978-1-4471-2161-9_17.

Cavicchi, D. (2014). Fandom before" fan": Shaping the history of enthusiastic audiences. Reception: Texts, Readers, Audiences, History, 6(1), 52-72. https://doi.org/10.5325/reception.6.1.0052

Chen, J. S. (2004). Mediating on the voiceless words of the invisible other: Young female anime fan artists-- narratives of gender images. *Social Theory in Art Education*, *24*(1), 213-233.

Chen, M. (2009). Communication, Coordination, and Camaraderie in World of Warcraft. *Games and Culture*, *4*(1), 47–73.

Cohen, E. (2010). Expectancy violations in relationships with friends and media figures. *Communication Research Reports*(27)2, 97-111

Cohen, J. (2009). Parasocial interaction and identification. In Mary B. Oliver & Robin Nabi, eds., Thousand Oaks, CA: *The Sage Handbook of Media Processes and Effects,* Sage, 223-236.

Cole, H., & Griffiths, M. D. (2007). Social Interactions in Massively Multiplayer Online Role-Playing Games. *Cyberpsychology and Behavior, 10*(4), 575–583. https://doi.org/10.1089/cpb.2007.9988

Cordell, B.R., Schwalb, R. J., & Wyatt, J. (2014). *Player's Handbook* (5th ed.). Renton, WA: Wizards of the Coast.

Cote, A. (2015). "I can defend myself": Women's strategies for coping with harassment while gaming online. *Games and Culture, 12*, 136-155.

Cover, J. G. (2010). *The creation of narrative in tabletop role-playing games*. Retrieved from http://public.eblib.com/choice/publicfullrecord.aspx?p=547921

Crawford, J., Perkins, C., Baker, R. (2019). *Dragon of Icespire Peak: Essentials Kit Rulebook* (5th ed.). Renton, WA: Wizards of the Coast.

Crawford, J., Wyatt, J., Schwalb, R. J., & Cordell, B. R. (2014). *Player's Handbook*. Wizards of the Coast.

D'Anastasio, C. (2017). Therapists are using dungeons and dragons to get kids to open up. *Kotaku*. Retrieved from https://kotaku.com/therapists-are-using-dungeons-dragons-to-get-kids-to-1794806159

D'Anastasio, C. (2019, January 18). As spreadsheet of accused abusers spreads, anime conventions get their MeToo movement. *Kotaku*. Retrieved from https://kotaku.com/as-spreadsheet-of-accused-abusers-spreads-anime-conven-1831879237.

Dalbey, A. (2018, December 21). Making fun of Twitch thots is still a thing, apparently. *The Daily Dot*. Retrieved from https://www.dailydot.com/parsec/xqc-felix-lengyel-twitch-thots.

Daniau, S. (2016). The Transformative Potential of Role-Playing Games: From Play Skills to Human Skills. *Simulation and Gaming, 47*, 423-444. doi: 10.1177/1046878116650765

Daniel E.S. & Westerman, D. (2017). Valar Morghulis (All Parasocial Men Must Die): Having nonfictional responses to a fictional character. *Communication* Research Reports.

Daniel, E.S., Crawford, E., & Westerman, D. (2018). Understanding the influence of Social Media Influencers: Using the Lens of Taylor's Strategy Wheel and Parasocial Interaction to Understand Online Vaping Communities. *The Journal of Interactive Advertising* https://doi.org/10.1080/15252019.2018.1488637

Davis, K. E., & Todd, M. J. (1985). Assessing friendship prototypes. Paradigm cases and relationship description. In S. W. Duck & D. Perlman (Eds.), Understanding personal relationships: An interdisciplinary approach (pp. 17–38). Beverly Hills, CA: Sage.

DeMatteo, F.J., Arter, P.S., Sworen-Parise, C., Fasciana, M., & Paulhamus, M.A. (2012). Social skills training for young adults with autism spectrum disorder: overview and implications for practice, *National Teacher Education Journal, 5(4)*, 57-65.

Diener, E., Wirtz, D., & Oishi, S. (2001). End effects of rated life quality: The James Dean Effect. Psychological Science, 12, 124–128.

Dossey, J. A., Mullis, I. V. S., Lindquist, M. M., & Chambers, D. L (1988) The Mathematics Report Card: Trends and achievement based on the 1986 National Assessment. Princeton: Educational Testing Service.

Ducheneaut, N., & Moore, R. (2005). More than just 'XP': learning social skills in massively multiplayer online games. *Interactive Technology and Smart Education, 2*(2), 89–100.

Ducheneaut, N., Yee, N., Nickell, E., & Moore, R. (2006). "Alone together?": exploring the social dynamics of massively multiplayer online games. In *SIGCHI conference on Human factors in computing systems*. New York, NY: ACM.

Elbein, A. (2017, May 24). The real reasons for Marvel comics' woes. *The Atlantic*. Retrieved from https://www.theatlantic.com/entertainment/archive/2017/05/the-real-reasons-for-marvel-comics-woes/527127/.

Emmons, R. A. & McCullough, M. E. (2003). Counting blessings versus burdens: An experimental investigation of gratitude and subjective well-being in daily life. Journal of Personality and Social Psychology, 84, (2), 377-389

Entertainment Software Association. (2018). *2018 sales, demographic and usage date. Essential facts about the computer and video game industry.*

Erikson, E. (1982). *The life cycle completed.* New York: W. W. Norton.

Eyal, K., & Dailey, R. (2012). Examining relationship maintenance in parasocial relationships. *Mass Communication and Society, 15*, 758-781.

Fan culture and popular media, 30-49. New York; London: Routledge.https://doi:10.4324/9780203181539

Fiske, J. (1992). The cultural economy of fandom. In L. A. Lewis (Ed.), The adoring audience:

Fox, J., & Tang, W. Y. (2016). Women's experiences with general and sexual harassment in online video games: Rumination, organizational responsiveness, withdrawal, and coping strategies. *New Media & Society, 19*, 1290-1307.

Francisco, E. (2018, February 9). Comicsgate is Gamergate's next horrible evolution. *Inverse.* Retrieved from https://www.inverse.com/article/41132-comicsgate-explained-bigots-milkshake-marvel-dc-gamergate.

Frankl, V. E. (2006). *Man's search for meaning.* Boston: Beacon Press.

Frey, N. & Fisher, D. (2004). Using Graphic Novels, Anime, and the Internet in an Urban High School. *The English Journal, 93*(3), 19-25.

Froh, J. J., Sefick, W. J., & Emmons, R. A. (2008). Counting blessings in early adolescents: An experimental study of gratitude and subjective well-being. Journal of School Psychology, 46, 213-233.

Fry, R. (2017) "It's becoming more common for young adults to live at home – and for longer stretches." Pew Research Center, Washington, D.C. (2016) https://www.pewresearch.org/fact-tank/2017/05/05/its-becoming-more-common-for-young-adults-to-live-at-home-and-for-longer-stretches/

Garcia, A. (2016). Teacher as Dungeon Master. In A. Byers & F. Crocco (Eds.), *The Role-playing society: Essays on the cultural influence of RPGs* (pp. 164–183). Jefferson, N.C.: McFarland & Company.

Garcia, A. (2017). Privilege, Power, and Dungeons & Dragons: How Systems Shape Racial and Gender Identities in Tabletop Role-Playing Games. *Mind, Culture & Activity, 24*(3), 232–246. https://doi.org/10.1080/10749039.2017.1293691

Gardner, K. (2018, September 23). Viral tweet about fandom gatekeeping proves we still have a male geek problem. *The Mary Sue.* Retrieved from https://www.themarysue.com/fandom-gatekeeping-male-geeks.

Ghuman, D., & Griffiths, M. D. (2012). A Cross-genre Study of Online Gaming: Player Demographics, Motivation for Play, and Social Interactions Among Players. *International Journal of Cyber Behavior, Psychology, and Learning, 2*(1), 13–29.

Giles, D. (2002). Parasocial interaction: A review of the literature and a model for future Research. *Media Psychology, 4,* 279–305.

Gleich, Uli (1996), Sind Fernsehpersonen die "Freunde" des Zuschauers? Ein Vergleich zwischen parasozialen und realen sozialen Beziehungen [Are TV personalities/characters "friends" of the viewers? A comparison between parasocial and real social relationships], in Fernsehen als "Beziehingskiste": Parasoziale beziehungen und interaktionen mit TV-personen [TV as "relationship crate": Parasocial rela- tionships and interactions with TV personalities/characters], P. Vorderer, ed., Opladen, Germany: Westdeutscher Verlag, 113–44.

Goffman, E. (2007). *The presentation of self in everyday life.* London: Penguin Books.

Granshaw, L. (2018). How Tabletop Games like Dungeons & Dragons can be Therapeutic for Players. *Syfy Wire.* Retrieved from https://www.syfy.com/syfywire/how-tabletop-games-like-dungeons-dragons-can-be-therapeutic-for-players

Gray, K. L., & Leonard, D. (2018). *Woke gaming: Digital challenges to oppression and social injustice.* Seattle: University of Washington Press.

Griepp, M. & Miller, J.J. (2018). Comics and graphic novel sales hit new high in 2018. Retrieved July 27th, 2019, from http://comichron.com

Griffiths, M. D. (2010). Computer game playing and social skills: a pilot study. *Aloma, 27*, 301–310.

Griffiths, M. D., Davies, M., & Chappell, D. (2003). Breaking the Stereotype: The Case of Online Gaming. *Cyberpsychology and Behavior, 6*(1), 81–91.

Hartmann, T. & Goldhoorn, C. (2011). Horton and Wohl revisited: Exploring viewers experience of parasocial interaction. *Journal of Communication, 61*, 1104-1121.

Haslam, S. A., Jetten, J., Postmes, T., & Haslam, C. (2009). Social Identity, Health and Well-Being: An Emerging Agenda for Applied Psychology. *Applied Psychology-An International Review-Psychologie appliquee-Revue internationale, 58*(1), 1-23.

Have Disney strike Star Wars Episode VII from the official canon. *Change.org*. Retrieved from https://www.change.org/p/the-walt-disney-company-have-disney-strike-star-wars-episode-viii-from-the-official-canon.

Hayes, J. (2013). Manga industry in Japan: Artist, schools and amateur manga. Retrieved July 27th, 2019, from http://factsanddetails.com

Herholz, S. C., Herholz, R. S., & Herholz, K. (2013). Non-pharmacological interventions and neuroplasticity in early stage alzheimer›s disease. *Expert Review of Neurotherapeutics, 13*(11), 1235-45. doi:http://dx.doi.org.tcsedsystem. idm.oclc.org/10.1586/14737175.2013.845086

Hermann, K. (2015). Field Theory and Working With Group Dynamics in Debriefing. *Simulation & Gaming*, 1046878115596100. https://doi.org/10.1177/1046878115596100

Hogg, Michael. (2000). Subjective Uncertainty Reduction through Self-categorization: A Motivational Theory of Social Identity Processes. *European Review of Social Psychology, 11*(1).

Honomichl, R. D., & Chen, Z. (2010). Relations as Rules: The Role of Attention in the Dimensional Change Card Sort Task. *Developmental Psychology, 47*, 50-60.

Hussain, Z., & Griffiths, M. (2009). The Attitudes, Feelings, and Experiences of Online Gamers: A Qualitative Analysis. *Cyberpsychology and Behavior, 12*(6), 747–753.

Illing, S. (2017, September 19). The woman at the center of #Gamergate gives zero fucks about her hates. *Vox*. Retrieved from https://www.vox.com/culture/2017/9/19/16301682/gamergate-alt-right-zoe-quinn-crash-override-interview.

Jakobsson, M., & Taylor, T. L. (2003). The Sopranos meets EverQuest: Social networking in massively multiplayer online games. In *2003 Digital Arts and Culture (DAC) conference* (pp. 90–91). Melbourne, Australia.

Jansz, J., & Tanis, M. (2007). Appeal of Playing Online First Person Shooter Games. *Cyberpsychology and Behavior, 10*(1), 133–136.

Jenkins, H. (2006). *Convergence culture: Where old and new media collide.* New York: New York University Press.

Joinson, A. (2001). Self-disclosure in computer-mediated communication: the role of self-awareness and visual anonymity. *European Journal of Social Psychology, 31*, 177–192.

Jones, W. H., & Burdette, M. P. (1994). Betrayal in close relationships. In A. L. Weber & J. Harvey (Eds.), Perspectives on close relationships (pp. 243–262). New York: Allyn & Bacon.

K, Ben (2019, Feb 6). Anime fan is now reporting from Antarctica, furthest anime pilgrimage site on Earth. Retrieved July 26th, 2019, from http://grapee.jp

Kain, E. (2017, December 21). No, Rey from 'Star Wars: The Last Jedi' is still not a Mary Sue. *Forbes*. Retrieved from https://www.forbes.com/sites/erikkain/2017/12/21/no-rey-from-star-wars-the-last-jedi-is-still-not-a-mary-sue/#9d1d7b945004.

Kaplan, A. (2019, February 20). Right-wing trolls attack Brie Larson and target *Captain Marvel* with negative reviews on Rotten Tomatoes. *Media Matters*. Retrieved from https://www.mediamatters.org/blog/2019/02/20/Right-wing-trolls-attack-Brie-Larson-and-target-Captain-Marvel-with-negative-reviews-on-Ro/222924.

Kasof, J. (1995). Explaining Creativity: The Attributional Perspective. *Creativity Research Journal, 8*(4), 311.

Kaye, L. K., Kowert, R., & Quinn, S. (2017). The role of social identity and online social capital on psychosocial outcomes in MMO players. *Computers in Human Behavior, 74,* 215–223.

Kaylor, Stefanie L. B., "Dungeons and Dragons and literacy: The role tabletop role-playing games can play in developing teenagers' literacy skills and reading interests" (2017). Graduate Research Papers. 215. https://scholarworks.uni.edu/grp/215

Kefir, N., & Corsini, R. J. (1974). Dispositional sets: A contribution to typology. *Journal of Individual Psychology, 30* (2), 163.

Kelly, K. D. (2014-2015). Hawk & Moor: The unofficial history of Dungeons and Dragons. Middletown, DE: Wonderland Imprints.

Kim-Prieto, Diener, E., Tamir, M., Scollon, C., & Diener, M. (2005). Integrating the diverse definitions of happiness: A time-sequential framework of subjective wellbeing. Journal of Happiness Studies, 6, 261-300.

Kim, E., Namkoong, K., Ku, T., & Kim, S. (2008). The relationship between online game addiction and aggression, self-control, and narcissistic personality traits. *European Psychiatry, 23*(3), 212–218. https://doi.org/10.1016/j.eurpsy.2007.10.010

Kim, H., Kim, K. M., & Nomura, S. (2016). The effect of group art therapy on older korean adults with neurocognitive disorders. The Arts in Psychotherapy, 47, 48-54. doi:http://dx.doi.org.tcsedsystem.idm.oclc.org/10.1016/j.aip.2015.11.002

Kitchen, P., Williams, A., & Chowhan, J. (2012). Sense of belonging and mental health in Hamilton, Ontario: An intra-urban analysis. *Social Indicators Research, 108,* 277-297. Retrieved from https://link.springer.com/article/10.1007/s11205-012-0066-0.

Klimmt, C., Hartmann, T. & Schramm, H. (2006). Parasocial interactions and relationships. In Jennings Bryant & Peter Vorderer. eds., Mahwah, NJ: *Psychology of entertainment*, Lawrence Erlbaum Associates, 291-313.

Kubik, E. (2012). Masters of technology: Defining and theorizing the hardcore/casual dichotomy in video game culture. In Gajjala, R., & Oh Y. J. (Eds.), *Cyberfeminism 2.0* (pp 135-152). New York: Peter Lang.

Kurniawan I, Kolopaking MS. Management of irritable bowel syndrome in the elderly. *Acta Medica Indonesiana.* 2014;46(2):138-147.

Lankoski, P., & Järvelä, S. (2012). An embodied cognition approach for understanding role-playing. *International Journal of Role-Playing, 6,* 18-32.

Lasley, J. (2017) *Fantasy in real life: Making Meaning from Vicarious Experience with a Tabletop Role-Playing Game Webcast* (unpublished pilot study). University of San Diego, San Diego, CA.

Lau, J.C., Gbinigie, A., DePass, T., Boccamazzo, R. & Thompson, C. (2019). *Gaming while other: Accessibility, diversity representation.* Presented September 30, 2019 at PAX West 2019 in Seattle, WA.

Laycock, J. P. (2015). *Dangerous Games: What the Moral Panic over Role-Playing Games Says about Play, Religion, and Imagined Worlds* (1st ed.). Oakland, CA: University of California Press

Leary, M., & Kowalski, R. (1995). *Social Anxiety.* New York: Guilford Press.

Lee, E. & Burunova, A. (2019). *Enter the anime.* United States: Netflix

Lemmens, J., Valkenburg, P., & Peter, J. (2011). Psychological causes and consequences of pathological gaming. *Computers in Human Behavior, 27*(1), 144–152. https://doi.org/10.1016/j.chb.2010.07.015

Leonard, D. & Thurman, T. (2018). Bleed-out on the brain: The neuroscience of character-to-player spillover in LARP. *International Journal of Role-Playing, 9,* 9-15.

Lévy, P. (1997). *Collective intelligence: Mankinds emerging world in cyberspace.* Cambridge, Mass: Perseus Books.

Linehan, M. (2015). DBT skills training manual (2nd ed.). New York, NY: The Guilford Press

Liu, M., & Peng, W. (2009). Cognitive and psychological predictors of the negative outcomes associated with playing MMOGs (massively multiplayer online games). *Computers in Human Behavior, 25*(6), 1306–1311. https://doi.org/10.1016/j.chb.2009.06.002

Lo, S., Wang, C., & Fang, W. (2005). Physical Interpersonal Relationships and Social Anxiety among Online Game Players. *Cyberpsychology and Behavior, 8*(1), 15–20. https://doi.org/10.1089/cpb.2005.8.15

Loporcaro, J. A., Ortega, C. R., & Egnoto, M. J. (2014). The hardcore scorecard: Defining, quantifying and understanding "hardcore" video game culture. Proceedings of the New York State Communication Association, (2013)7, 1-15.

Lucas, K., & Sherry, J. (2004). Sex Differences in Video Game Play: A Communication-Based Explanation. *Communication Research, 31*(5), 499–523.

Lueck, J. (2015). Friend-zone with benefits: The parasocial advertising of Kim Kardashian. *Journal of Marketing Communications, 21*(2), 91-109.

Luo, L., PhD., & Craik, F. I. M., PhD. (2008). Aging and memory: A cognitive approach. Canadian Journal of Psychiatry, 53(6), 346-53. Retrieved from https://tcsedsystem.idm.oclc.org/login?url=https://search-proquest-com.tcsedsystem.idm.oclc.org/docview/222797444?accountid=34120

Lyubomirsky, S., King, L., & Diener, E. (2005). The benefits of frequent positive affect: Does happiness lead to success? Psychological Bulletin, 131 (6), 803-855.

Lyubomirsky, S., Sheldon, K. M, & Schkade, D. (2005). Pursuing happiness: The architecture of sustainable change. Review of General Psychology, 9(2), 111-131. Retrieved from https://escholarship.org/uc/item/4v03h9gv

MacLeod, A. K., Coates, E., & Hetherton, J. (2008). Increasing well-being through teaching goal-setting and planning skills: Results of a brief intervention. Journal of Happiness Studies, 9, 18-196.

Macwilliams, M. W. (2008). *Japanese visual culture: Explorations in the world of manga and anime.* Armonk, N.Y: M.E. Sharpe.

Maslow, A. H. (1973). Self-actualizing people: A study of psychological health. In R. J. Lowry (Ed.), *Dominance, self-esteem, self-actualization: Germinal papers of A. H. Maslow* (pp. 177-201). Monterey, CA: Brookes/Cole Publishing Company. (Original work published in 1950).

Massanari, A. L. (2015). Participatory culture, community, and play: Learning from Reddit. New York: Peter Lang.

Matz, S., Chan, Y.W.F., & Kosinski, M. (2016). Models of personality. In Tkalčič, M., De Carolis, B., de Gemmis, M., Odić, A., & Košir, A. (eds) *Emotions and Personality in Personalized Services.* Springer, Cham, Switzerland. 35-54.

McArthur, J. A. (2009). Digital Subculture: A Geek Meaning of Style. *Journal of Communication Inquiry, 33*(1), 58–70. https://doi.org/10.1177/0196859908325676

McCullough, M. E., Pargament, K. I., & Thoresen, C. E. (2000). The psychology of forgiveness: History, conceptual issues, and overview. In M. E. McCullough, K. I. Pargament, & C. E. Thoresen (Eds.), Forgiveness: Theory, research, and practice (p. 1–14). Guilford Press

McCutcheon, L., Lange, R., Houran, J. (2002). Conceptualization and measure of celebrity worship. *British Journal of Psychology,* 93, 67-87.

McKenna, K., & Bargh, J. (2000). Plan 9 from cyberspace: The implications of the Internet for personality and social psychology. *Personality and Social Psychology Review, 4*(1), 57–75. https://doi.org/10.1207/S15327957PSPR0401_6

McLean, L., & Griffiths, M. D. (2018). Female gamers' experiences of online harassment and social support in online gaming: A qualitative study. *International Journal of Mental Health and Addiction.* doi.org/10.1007/s11469-018-9962-0

Mearls, M, Crawford, J., Perkins, C., Wyatt, J., Thompson, R., Schwalb, S., Lee, P, Townshend, S., Cordell, B. (2014). *Lost Mines of Phandelver: Starter Set Rulebook* (5th ed.). Renton, WA: Wizards of the Coast.

Medvec, V. H., Madey, S. F., & Gilovich, T. (1995). When less is more: Counterfactual thinking and satisfaction among Olympic medalists. *Journal of Personality and Social Psychology, 69,* 603–610.

Moore, J. C. (2002). Comment: Copyright Protection or Fan Loyalty-Must Entertainment Companies Choose? Alternate Solutions for Addressing Internet Fan Sites. *North Carolina Journal of Law & Technology, 3*(2), 273-304. Retrieved February 19, 2019, from http://ncjolt.org/wp-content/uploads/2016/09/18_3NCJLTech2732001-2002.pdf

Moore, R., Ducheneaut, N., & Nickell, E. (2007). Doing Virtually Nothing: Awareness and Accountability in Massively Multiplayer Online Worlds. *Computer Supported Cooperative Work, 16*(3), 265–305.

Nabi, R., Biely, E. N., Morgan, S. J., & Stitt, C. R. (2003). Reality-based television programming and the psychology of its appeal. *Media Psychology, 5*(4), 303–330

Nguyen, L., Murphy, K., & Andrews, G. (2019). Immediate and long-term efficacy of executive functions cognitive training in older adults: A systematic review and meta-analysis. Psychological Bulletin, doi:http://dx.doi.org.tcsedsystem.idm.oclc.org/10.1037/bul0000196

Noble, G. (1975). *Children in Front of the Small Screen.* Beverly Hills, Calif.: Sage.

Nordlund, J. (1978). Media interaction. *Communication Research, 5,* 150–175.

Norman, R. (2012). Music therapy assessment of older adults in nursing homes. Music Therapy Perspectives, 30(1), 8-16. Retrieved from https://tcsedsystem.idm.oclc.org/login?url=https://search-proquest-com.tcsedsystem.idm.oclc.org/docview/1041061474?accountid=34120

O'Leary, A. (2012, August 1). In virtual play, sex harassment is all too real. *The New York Times.* Retrieved from https://www.nytimes.com/2012/08/02/us/sexual-harassment-in-online-gaming-stirs-anger.html.

Oestriecher, B. (2018, December 02). 5 Huge Heel Turns WWE Must Pull Off ASAP. Retrieved February 19, 2019, from https://web.archive.org/web/20181203213509/https://www.forbes.com/sites/blakeoestriecher/2018/12/02/5-huge-heel-turns-wwe-must-pull-off-asap/

Oldenburg, R. (1999). *The Great Good Place: Cafés, Coffee Shops, Community Centers, Beauty Parlors, General Stores, Bars, Hangouts, and How They Get You Through The Day.* New York: Marlowe & Company.

Olson, C. J. (2018). *100 Greatest Cult Films.* Lanham, MA: Rowman & Littlefield.

Ong, T. (2017, December 24). In The Last Jedi, being a space cowboy doesn't fly anymore. *The Verge.* Retrieved from https://www.theverge.com/2017/12/24/16766588/the-last-jedi-poe-dameron-star-wars.

Orme, S. (2016). Femininity and fandom: The dual-stigmatization of female comic book fans. *The Journal of Graphic Novels and Comics 7*(4), 403-416. doi: 10.1080/21504857.2016.1219958

Owen, A. M., Hampshire, A., Grahn, J. A., Stenton, R., Dajani, S., Burns, A. S., ... Ballard, C. G. (2010). Putting brain training to the test. Nature, 465(7299), 775–778. doi:10.1038/nature09042

Papp KV, Walsh SJ, Snyder PJ. Immediate and delayed effects of cognitive interventions in healthy elderly: a review of current literature and future directions. Alzheimers Dement. 2009;5:50–60.

Pavlas, D., Bedwell, W., Wooten, S. R., Heyne, K., & Salas, E. (2009). Investigating the Attributes in Serious Games that Contribute to Learning. *Proceedings of the Human Factors and Ergonomics Society Annual Meeting, 53*(27), 1999–2003. https://doi.org/10.1177/154193120905302705

Peters, C., & Malesky, A. (2008). Problematic Usage Among Highly-Engaged Players of Massively Multiplayer Online Role Playing Games. *Cyberpsychology and Behavior, 11*(4), 481–484.

Petrakovitz, C. (2018, November 19). Watch every Marvel movie *and* show in the perfect order. Retrieved February 18, 2019, from https://web.archive.org/

web/20190212132219/https://www.cnet.com/how-to/marvel-cinematic-universe-timeline-order-avengers-4/

Planalp, S., & Honeycutt, J. (1985). Events that increase uncertainty in personal relationships. Human Communication Research, 11, 593–604.

Proctor, C. L., Linley, P. A., & Maltby, J. (2009). Youth life satisfaction: A review of the literature. Journal of Happiness Studies, 10, 583-630.

Qu, L., & Zelazo, P. D. (2007). The facilitative effect of positive stimuli on 3-year-olds' flexible rule use. *Cognitive Development, 22*, 456-473. doi: 10.1016/j.cogdev.2007.08.010

Rachel, W. & Turkot, A. (2014). Psychotherapy in older adults with major depression in psychogeriatric ward. Psychoterapia. 171. 77-87. Doi: 10.12740/PT/30178.

Ray, A., Plante, C. N., Reysen, S., Roberts, S. E., & Gerbasi, K. C. (2017). Psychological needs predict The Phoenix Papers, Vol. 4, No. 1, August 2018 37 fanship and fandom in anime fans. The Phoenix Papers, 3, 56-68.

Reagle, J. (2015). Geek policing: Fake geek girls and contested attention. *The International Journal of Communication, 9*, 2862-2880.

Reichow, B., Steiner, A. M., & Volkmar, F. R. (2013). Cochrane review: social skills groups for people aged 6 to 21 with autism spectrum disorders (ASD). *Evidence-Based Child Health a Cochrane Review Journal, 8*(2), 266–315. doi: 10.1002/ebch.1903.

Reynor, F. (2017). Four ways in which anime impacts culture and influences male fans [Blog Post]. Retrieved from: https://goodmenproject.com/guy-talk/4-ways-in-which-anime-impacts-culture-and-influences-male-fans-wcz/

Riesman, A. (2017, June 27). First Captain America Became Evil, Then the Comics World Erupted. Retrieved February 19, 2019, from https://web.archive.org/web/20181202044414/https://www.vulture.com/2017/06/marvel-hydra-captain-america-nick-spencer.html

Rivers, A., Wickramasekera, I. E. II, Pekala, R. J., & Rivers, J. A. (2016). Empathic Features and Absorption in Fantasy Role-Playing. *American Journal of Clinical Hypnosis, 58*, 286-294. doi: 10.1080/00029157.2015.1103696

Robertson, I. H. (2013). A noradrenergic theory of cognitive reserve: implications for Alzheimer's disease. Neurobiol. Aging 34, 298–308. doi: 10.1016/j.neurobiolaging.2012.05.019

Robinson, M. (2018, October 05). Why Wearing Your Team's Jersey is the Only Socially Acceptable Cosplay. Retrieved February 17, 2019, from https://web.archive.org/web/20190217172454/https://melmagazine.com/en-us/story/why-wearing-your-teams-jersey-is-the-only-socially-acceptable-cosplay

Rogers, Carl (1951). *Client-Centered Therapy*. Cambridge Massachusetts: The Riverside Press.

Rosaen, S. & Dibble, J. (2008). Investigating the relationships among child's age, parasocial interaction, and the social realism of favorite television characters, *Communication Research Reports, 25*(2), 145-154.

Rose, R., & Anketell, C. (2009). The Benefits of Social Skills Groups for Young People with Autism Spectrum Disorder: A Pilot Study. *Child Care in Practice, 15*(2), 127–144. https://doi.org/10.1080/13575270802685377

Rosenberg, R. S. (2010, August 6). Comic-Con: Nerd and Geek Community. Retrieved June 6, 2019, from https://www.psychologytoday.com/us/blog/the-superheroes/201008/comic-con-nerd-and-geek-community

Rothenbuhler, E. W. (1998). *Ritual communication: From everyday conversation to mediated ceremony*. Thousand Oaks, CA: Sage.

Rubin, L., & Livesay, H. (2006). Look, up in the sky! Using superheroes in play therapy. *International Journal of Play Therapy, 15*(1), 117-133. doi:10.1037/h0088911

Rubinstein, J. S., Meyer, D. E., & Evans, E. (2001). Executive Control of Cognitive Processes in Task Switching. *Journal of Experimental Psychology, 27*, 763-797. doi: 10.1037//0096-1523.27.4.763

Schmid, W., & Ostermann, T. (2010). Home-based music therapy - a systematic overview of settings and conditions for an innovative service in healthcare. BMC Health Services Research, 10, 291. doi:http://dx.doi.org.tcsedsystem.idm.oclc.org/10.1186/1472-6963-10-29

Schodt, F. L. (1996). *Dreamland Japan: Writings on modern manga.*

Schramm, H. and Hartmann, T. (2008). The PSI-process scales: A new measure to assess the intensity and breadth of parasocial processes. *Communications: The European Journal of Communication Research, 33*(4), 385-401.

Scott, S. (2017). #Wheresrey?: Toys, spoilers, and the gender politics of franchise paratexts. *Critical Studies in Media Communication, 34,* 138-147.

Scott, S. (2019). *Fake geek girls: Fandom, gender, and the convergence culture industry.* New York: NYU Press.

Segrin, C., & Kinney, T. (1995). Social skills deficits among the socially anxious: Loneliness and rejection from others. *Motivation and Emotion,* (19), 1–24.

Seligman, M. E. P., & Csikszentmihalyi, M. (2000). Positive psychology introduction. American Psychologist, 55, 5-14.

Seligman, M. E. P., Steen, T. A., Park, N., & Peterson, C. (2005). Positive Psychology Progress: Empirical validation of interventions. American Psychologist, 60, (5), 410-421.

Sheldon, K. M., Kasser, T., Smith, K., & Share, T. (2002). Personal goals and psychological growth: Testing an intervention to enhance goal attainment and personality integration. Journal of Personality, 70, 5-31.

Shen, C., & Williams, D. (2010). Unpacking Time Online: Connecting Internet and Massively Multiplayer Online Game Use With Psychological Well-Being. *Communication Research, 20*(10), 1–27. https://doi.org/10.1177/0093650210377196

Smyth, J. M., Johnson, J. A., Auer, B. J., Lehman, E., Talamo, G., & Sciamanna, C. N. (2018). Online Positive Affect Journaling in the Improvement of Mental Distress and Well-Being in General Medical Patients With Elevated Anxiety Symptoms: A Preliminary Randomized Controlled Trial. *JMIR mental health, 5*(4), e11290. doi:10.2196/11290

Snyder, C. R., Rand, K. L., & Sigmon, D. R. (2005). Hope theory: A member of the positive psychology family. In C. R. Snyder & S. J. Lopez (Eds.), Handbook of Positive Psychology (pp. 257-276). New York: Oxford University Press, Inc.

Steiner, R. J., Sheremenko, G., Lesesne, C., Dittus, P. J., Sieving, R. E., & Ethier, K. A. (2019). Adolescent Connectedness and Adult Health Outcomes. Pediatrics, 144(1), e20183766. doi:10.1542/peds.2018-3766

Steinkuehler, C., & Williams, D. (2006). Where Everybody Knows Your (Screen) Name: Online Games as "Third Places." *Journal of Computer-Mediated Communication, 11*(4), 885–909.

Stephenson, R. C. (2013). Promoting well-being and gerotranscendence in an art therapy program for older adults. Art Therapy, 30(4), 151-158. Doi:10.1080/07421 656.2014.846206

Strack, F., Schwarz, N., & Gschneidinger, E. (1985). Happiness and reminiscing: The role of time perspective, affect, and mode of thinking. Journal of Personality and Social Psychology, 49, 1460–1469.

Suldo, S. M., Huebner, E. S., Savage, J., & Thalji, A. (2010). Promoting subjective well-being. In M. A. Bray, T. J. Kehle, & P.E. Nathan (Eds.), The Oxford Handbook of School Psychology (pp. 504-522). Oxford University Press: New York.

Suler, J. (2004). The Online Disinhibition Effect. *Cyberpsychology and Behavior, 7*(3), 321–326.

Suskind, A. (2014, February 17). The Rise of Superhero Therapy: Comic Books as Psychological Treatment. Retrieved February 19, 2019, from https://web.archive.org/web/20181229220637/https://www.thedailybeast.com/the-rise-of-superhero-therapy-comic-books-as-psychological-treatment

Tajfel, H. (1970). Experiments in intergroup discrimination. *Scientific American, 223*(2), 96–102.

Tajfel, H. (1978). The achievement of group differentiation BT - Differentiation between soical groups. STudies in the social psychology of intergroup relations. In *Differentiation between soical groups. Studies in the social psychology of intergroup relations.* (pp. 77–98). Longon: Academic Press.

Tajfel, H., & Turner, J. C. (1979). An Integrative Theory of Intergroup Conflict BT - The Social Psychology of Intergroup Relations. In W. G. Austin & S. Worchel (Eds.), *The Social Psychology of Intergroup Relations* (pp. 33–47). Monterey: Brooks-Cole.

Tajfel, H., & Turner, J. C. (1985). The social identity theory of intergroup behavior BT - Psychology of Intergroup Relations. In S. Worcehl & W. G. Austin (Eds.), *Psychology of Intergroup Relations*. Chicago: Nelson-Hall.

Talbott, C. (2019). Bam! Pow! Women rule at Emerald City Comic Con. *Seattle Times*. Retrieved from seattletimes.com/entertainment/events/bam-pow-women-rule-at-emerald-city-comic-con/

Tedeschi, R. G., & Calhoun, L. G. (2004). Target Article: "Posttraumatic Growth: Conceptual Foundations and Empirical Evidence". *Psychological Inquiry, 15*(1), 1–18

Throsby, D. (2011). Cultural capital. *A Handbook of Cultural Economics,* 142-146. doi:10.4337/9781781008003.00025

Tilton, S. (2014, August 22). Mobile Public Memory: The (Digital/Physical) (Artifacts/Souvenirs) of the (Archiver/Tourist). *SAGE Open, 4*(3), 1-11. doi:10.1177/2158244014547324

Tilton, S. (2016, June 15). The Four Temperaments of Fandom. Retrieved February 17, 2019, from https://www.academia.edu/26449531/The_Four_Temperaments_of_Fandom

Tilton, S. (2019). Winning Through Deception: A Pedagogical Case Study on Using Social Deception Games to Teach Small Group Communication Theory. *SAGE Open, 9*(1), 2158244019834370. https://doi.org/10.1177/2158244019834370

Tocci, J. (2009). Geek cultures: Media and identity in the digital age. Ph.D. dissertation. University of Pennsylvania.

Toles-Patkin, T. (1986). Rational Coordination in the Dungeon. *The Journal of Popular Culture, 20*(1), 1–14. https://doi.org/10.1111/j.0022-3840.1986.2001_1.x

Towse, J. N., Redbond, J., Houston-Price, C. M. T., & Cook, S. (2000). Understanding the dimensional change card sort: Perspectives from task success and failure. *Cognitive Development, 15,* 347-365. doi: 10.1016/S0885-2014(00)00021-6

Tran, K.M. (2018). Kelly Marie Tran: I won't be marginalized by online harassment. *The New York Times.* Retrieved from https://www.nytimes.com/2018/08/21/movies/kelly-marie-tran.html

Tse, M. M. Y., Lau, J. K. L., Kwan, R., Cheung, D., Tang, A. S. K., Ng, S. S. M., ... Yeung, S. S. Y. (2018). Effects of play activities program for nursing home residents with dementia on pain and psychological well-being: Cluster randomized controlled trial. *Geriatrics & Gerontology International, 18*(10), 1485–1490. https://doi-org.tcsedsystem.idm.oclc.org/10.1111/ggi.13509

Turner, J. C. (1984). Social identification and psychological group formation BT - The social dimension. In H. Tajfel (Ed.), *The social dimension* (Vol. 2, pp. 518–538). Cambridge: Cambridge University Press.

Tyson J (2013). "Turning a tragedy into a tribute: A literature review of creating meaning after loss of a loved one". Illness, Crisis, & Loss. **21**(4): 325–340. doi:10.2190/IL.21.4.e.

Vignoles, V. L., Regalia, C., Manzi, C., Golledge, J., & Scabini, E. (2006). Beyond self-esteem: Influence of multiple motives on identity construction. *Journal of Personality and Social Psychology, 90,* 308-333. doi:10.1037/0022-3514.90.2.308

Vorderer, P., Hartmann, T., & Klimmt, C. (2003). Explaining the enjoyment of playing video games: the role of competition. In *Proceedings of the second international conference on Entertainment computing*.

Vorderer, P., Klimmt, C. & Ritterfeld, U. (2004). Enjoyment: At the heart of media entertainment. *Communication Theory, 14*(4), 388-408.

Vygotsky, L. S. (1978). *Mind in society: the development of higher psychological processes* (M. Cole, ed.). Cambridge, Mass: Harvard Univ. Press.

Waldman, K. (2014, June 3). Comic-con International has no interest in taking on sexual harassment. *Slate*. Retrieved from https://slate.com/human-interest/2014/06/sexual-harassment-at-comic-con-san-diego-convention-says-no-to-a-more-comprehensive-policy.html.

Walsh, D. (2016, May 31). Fans Protest The 'Captain America' Controversy Through Positivity. Retrieved February 19, 2019, from https://web.archive.org/web/20170317145443/http://uproxx.com/gammasquad/captain-america-fans-holocaust-museum/

Walther, J. (1996). Computer-mediated communication: Impersonal, interpersonal, and hyperpersonal interaction. *Communication Research, 23*(1), 3–43.

Walther, J., Kashian, N., Jang, J.W., Shin, S.Y, Dai, Y., & Koutamanis, M. (2018). The effect of message persistence and disclosure on liking in Computer Mediated Communication. *Media Psychology*, 21(2), 308 – 327.

Wann, D. L. (2006). Understanding the positive social psychological benefits of sport team identification: The Team Identification--Social Psychological Health Model. Group Dynamics: Theory, Research, and Practice, 10, 272-296.

Whitty, M., & Gavin, J. (2001). Age/Sex/Location: Uncovering the Social Cues in the Development of Online Relationships. *Cyberpsychology and Behavior, 4*(5), 623–630.

Williams, J. P., Hendricks, S. Q., & Winkler, W. K. (Eds.). (2006). *Gaming as culture: essays on reality, identity and experience in fantasy games*. Jefferson, N.C: McFarland & Co.

Williams, Kristine N.,R.N., PhD., & Kemper, S., PhD. (2010). Interventions to reduce cognitive decline in aging. Journal of Psychosocial Nursing & Mental Health Services, 48(5), 42-51. doi:http://dx.doi.org.tcsedsystem.idm.oclc.org/10.3928/02793695-20100331-03

Wilson, T. D., Meyers, J., & Gilbert, D. T. (2003). "How happy was I, anyway?" A retrospective impact bias. Social Cognition, 21, 421–446.

Wingfield, N. (2014, October 15). Feminist critics of video games facing threats in 'Gamergate' campaign. *The New York Times*. Retrieved from https://www.nytimes.com/2014/10/16/ technology/gamergate-women- video-game-threats-anita-sarkeesian.html.

Winnicott, D. W. (1989). *Playing and reality*. London ; New York: Routledge.

Wirtz, D., Kruger, J., Scollon, C. N., & Diener, E. (2004). What to do on spring break? Predicting future choice from online versus recalled affect. Psychological Science, 14, 520–524.

Wolf, M. J. P. (2002). Genre and the video game. *The Medium of the Video Game*.

Yalom, I. D., & Leszcz, M. (2005). *The theory and practice of group psychotherapy* (5th ed). New York: Basic Books.

Yates, T.M., Tyrell, F., & Masten, A.S. (2014). Resilience theory and the practice of positive psychology from individuals to societies. In S. Joseph (Eds.), Positive psychology in practice: Promoting human flourishing in work, health, education, and everyday life (pp. 773-788). Retrieved from https://doi.org/10.1002/9781118996874.ch44

Yee, N. (2002). Befriending Ogres and Wood-Elves -Understanding Relationship Formation in MMORPGs. *Nickyee.Com*. Retrieved from http://www.nickyee.com/hub/relationships/home.html

Yee, N. (2007). Motivations of Play in Online Games. *Journal of CyberPsychology and Behavior, 9*(6), 772–775.

Zayas, L. H., & Lewis, B. H. (1986). Fantasy Role-Playing for Mutual Aid in Children's Groups. *Social Work with Groups, 9*(1), 53–66. https://doi.org/10.1300/J009v09n01_05

Zimmerman, E. (2002). Do independent games exist? In L. King (Ed.), *Game on: The history and culture of video games*. New York: Universe Publishing.